LIFE UNDER THE PALMS

LIFE UNDER THE PALMS

The Sublime World of the Anti-colonialist Jacob Haafner

PAUL VAN DER VELDE

Translated by Liesbeth Bennink

RIDGE BOOKS
SINGAPORE

Published under the Ridge Books imprint by:

NUS Press
National University of Singapore
AS3-01-02
3 Arts Link
Singapore 117569

Fax: (65) 6774-0652
E-mail: nusbooks@nus.edu.sg
Website: http://nuspress.nus.edu.sg

ISBN 978-981-325-082-6 (paper)

National Library Board, Singapore Cataloguing in Publication Data

Name(s): Velde, Paul van der. | Bennink, Liesbeth, translator.
Title: Life under the palms : the sublime world of the anti-colonialist Jacob Haafner / Paul van der Velde ; translated by Liesbeth Bennink.
Description: Singapore : Ridge Books, [2020]
Identifier(s): OCN 1090201311 | ISBN 978-981-3250-82-6 (paperback)
Subject(s): LCSH: Haafner, Jacob. | Travelers--Netherlands--Biography.
Classification: DDC 910.92--dc23

Cover image: From *Reize in eenen Palanquin*, vol. 2 (Amsterdam 1808). Jacob Haafner and Mamia, his Indian girlfriend, are reunited at the tank of the temple of Nawabpet.

Typeset by: Ogma Solutions Pvt Ltd
Printed by: Markono Print Media Pte Ltd

Dedicated to my Haafner brother

Jaap de Moor

Fig. 1 From *Reize in eenen Palanquin*, vol. 2 (Amsterdam 1808). A (nose) flute player.

Contents

Contents

List of Illustrations

List of Illustrations

An Introduction

Haafner's Journeys

Jacob Gotfried Haafner (1754–1809) lived in South Africa, Java, Sri Lanka, India, and Mauritius for more than 20 years. He wrote five accounts of his travels there, in which the colonial environment was not spared his strong criticism. Haafner wrote a provocative treatise on the havoc wrought by missionaries and missionary societies worldwide, from which he inferred that missionaries were not needed overseas as "the natives were happy as they were" and, in most cases, were more cultured than these promoters of the so-called "Western civilization". Haafner was ostracized by his fellow Dutch citizens after the publication of this essay because he had dared to consider non-Western people not only as his equals but even as his superiors.

However, there was certainly another, lighter, side to his writings. Indeed, his direct, gripping style of writing and his adventurous life made him one of the most popular Dutch writers of the early nineteenth century. His five travel books are among the best travel writing in Dutch of the whole colonial era, and remain of interest to this very day. The vivid descriptions of everyday life in the tropics bear testimony to his sharp powers of observation. His books won much acclaim in the early days of Romanticism and were immediately translated into German, French, Danish, Swedish, and English.

Haafner was deeply in love with Indian culture. He studied the languages and cultures of the subcontinent and was delighted when mistaken for an Indian. He is said to have been the first Dutchman with a genuine interest in India and its people and as a result became a diehard Anglophobe. "Had I to write the history of the English and their deeds in Asia", Haafner once wrote, "it would be the spitting image of Hell". Corruption, plunder, murder: everything seemed to be acceptable in the eyes of that despicable nation. The English did not even hesitate to cause famine in their Asian colonies for love of gain, as will be illustrated later on.

Exiled from his heart's desire and living under the grey skies of Amsterdam around the turn of the nineteenth century, India's reality became even more present in his writings. He tried to sell his treatises on Indian gods, rites and dancers to the erudite Dutch Society of Sciences; but Dutch scholars were neither interested in them, nor in his drawings of Mamia, his Indian lover, which they regarded as provocative. Fortunately these drawings have survived the passage of time as gaily colored and detailed engravings in his books.

The degree to which Haafner was in love with India is also betrayed by the fact that he wanted to publish a journal devoted solely to India. In the Amsterdam of his day, however, nobody was interested in India; no one that is, except for a young German, A.W. Schlegel. While there is no hard evidence to prove the point, it is very likely that they met in one of the many Amsterdam coffee shops, perhaps the Bird of Paradise, known as a meeting place for intellectuals. Schlegel was then a teacher in the employ of a rich banking family. He was later to become famous as a philosopher, critic and translator, the leading advocate of Romanticism and the study of India in German-speaking countries.

Haafner's five extensive travelogues constituted a sort of autobiography in five parts, and were written in the period between 1795 and 1809, a time in which the Netherlands was a loyal ally to the French and a kingdom under the rule of the French king, Louis Napoleon, brother of the Emperor. The French remained in control until 1813; by that time, Haafner was dead.

When Haafner published his first book, in 1806, he was living in poverty; in fact, he was completely down and out. He had done everything he possibly could to find work, or to attract the attention of the authorities. Being anti-English was a useful tool to achieve that aim. He condemned with anger and passion the loss of the Dutch trading emporium in Asia. He deplored the easy way in which the English has succeeded in capturing the factories of the Dutch East India Company (VOC) and territories in Sri Lanka, India, and South Africa.

In 1796, at the age of 42, Haafner applied for a job with the directors of the Dutch East India Company. He was thinking of a job on the Board of Directors. Was this asking too much? Given his many skills such a high function would do him justice, so he felt. In his letter to the directors he recommended himself as follows:

> Diligence, zeal, an intimate knowledge of Dutch, French, German, Portuguese, Hindi, Tamil, and English (yes, indeed!) and of bookkeeping; an excellent style of writing, a thorough knowledge of the religions and trade of India.

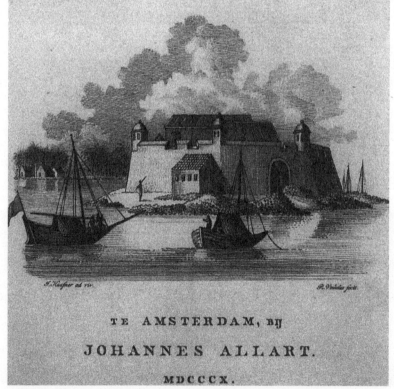

R E I Z E

TE VOET DOOR HET EILAND

C E I L O N.

DOOR

J. HAAFNER.

MET PLAATEN.

in een Boekdeel.

J. Haafner ad viv. *R. Vinkeles fecit.*

TE AMSTERDAM, BIJ

JOHANNES ALLART.

MDCCCX.

Fig. 2 Frontispiece of *Reize te voet door het Eiland Ceilon* (Amsterdam 1810).

These were no insignificant qualities, and what is more, it was true. The directors were less convinced, and his requests were turned down without much ado, leaving him, as he wrote in an angry letter to them, facing "a sad and desperate prospect". And it was a sad and desperate prospect. After many wonderful years spent in Asia as a servant of the VOC, as a private trader and traveler, he now had to live in Amsterdam, a gloomy and miserable city afflicted with a severe economic crisis and covered by an everlasting, thick, and depressing layer of clouds. A horrible city:

> No, in Europe and especially in its northern climes, no one enjoys their life. It is safe to say that their life withers away. In a word, they die without having ever truly lived.

Haafner, it is clear, suffered from an acute and incurable nostalgia for Asia while living in Europe.

Thirty years before, in 1766, as a 12-year-old boy, he had departed to Asia for the first time. After a short stay in Amsterdam, he again left for Asia in 1771, now 17 years old, to stay in India almost without interruption until 1787. From 1790, at the age of 36, he lived in Amsterdam till his death in 1809; 19 difficult and probably unsatisfactory years, which were spent dreaming of India and writing on his life and adventures there. At first he must have lived in relative prosperity. In India he had collected—in good colonial fashion—a modest fortune by participating in the flourishing diamond trade. After his return to Europe he had, however, made a big mistake (apart from returning): he invested his money in French state certificates. After the French Revolution the value of the bonds collapsed with lightning speed. Soon after 1790, Haafner had to eke out a meager livelihood as a shopkeeper selling pipes.

In the next years he moved a number of times from one address to another, and life did not get any better. He felt frustrated and misunderstood; he missed having a job, a social position, and he lacked the social status so as to be included as a member of the scholarly or literary societies in the city, to which he felt himself entitled. Apart from that, he suffered from a deteriorating health because he was increasingly tormented by angina pectoris, which would ultimately lead to his death. From 1791 on, he was responsible for a family with three children. Shortly before his death he married his wife officially; they had been together since 1790.

He probably filled his days visiting coffee houses (does anything ever change in Amsterdam?), meeting people from abroad in the harbor city, and with writing and coming up with new plots for books and journals. He worked on a translation of the Sanskrit Ramayana epic (which was published posthumously by his eldest son in the 1820s), and he prepared the publication of a treatise on the harmful consequences of the Christian missions in the overseas world, which was published in 1807.

Haafner's five entertaining travel books published between 1806 and 1821—partly during his life, partly posthumously—were what made him truly unique. They describe his many exciting adventures and colorful encounters, situated in India in the declining years of the VOC, in a lively and sparkling style and manner. The publication of these travelogues made him instantly famous, and he finally received the recognition he deserved. It is only a pity he did not have long to enjoy his fame.

The books were translated into German, French, English, Danish, and Swedish. In Germany he was praised for giving such good information on the culture and people of India. The French considered him a real intellectual: *"un penseur original et profound, qui a rendu ses idées dans un style aussi brilliant que énergique"*. But the nicest comment undoubtedly came from an English reviewer. In a rare combination of generosity and insult he wrote: "There is an air of sprightliness about Mr. Haafner, which certainly belies the place of his nativity." It had probably escaped the notice of the reviewer that Haafner was not born in Holland, but in Halle in Germany.

Haafner and His Times

The central theme of Haafner's travel writing is his life in India, his travels in that country, his contacts with the inhabitants, the customs of the people, and the landscape. What image does he present of it? Haafner adored India; he idealized the country and its people. By way of contrast, he criticized the Europeans there—primarily the English—for causing havoc and suffering among the local populations. The Europeans are invariably Haafner's villians. They turned Asia into a European penal colony:

> Rascals, squanderers, criminals, bankrupts, and other bad people: every one runs to the Indies, to oppress the poor Indians, to plunder them, and to kill them.

No other contemporary writer ever criticized colonialism more adamantly and more vehemently than Jacob Haafner did.

The Indians, in turn, are praised for their noble and humanitarian way of life. Haafner read Jean-Jacques Rousseau, praised the ideal of vegetarianism and severely disliked hunting and the killing of animals. He converted to vegetarianism himself and gave up hunting although he had been, until the moment of his conversion, an ardent hunter.

Haafner also admired the Indian princes, especially Haidar Ali, the monarch of Mysore. It was he who was wrecking the power of the English in India. He was depicted by Haafner as a freedom fighter, almost in the same manner as twentieth-century intellectuals once admired Fidel Castro as the lonely, heroic fighter against US imperialism.

Haafner was proud of almost being an Indian among the Indians. He saw himself blending in with his Indian environment; fusing with India and its inhabitants. What he liked most was not being recognized as a European or a white man.

> I had to laugh that this man mistook me for a mestizo. It is true,
> I entirely had the attitude and appearance of a mestizo. Not only
> was I without socks and shoes, but my face was burnt by the sun
> and I spoke the Tamil language fluently and properly.

What Haafner describes in his stories are the mixed, international communities of Indians, other Asians, Europeans of various nationalities and *mestizos*, inhabiting the coastal regions of India in which he himself lived with such ease and pleasure. The small city of Sadras, where he worked for two years until the English conquest, is depicted in all its colorful aspects. What he liked was the absence of any form of pretentiousness, ceremonialism, and conventionalism, so typical of Dutch society, where everything was organized according to hierarchy and status. In Sadras he lived in a socially mixed society, with parties and picnics at night, in an exuberant and elated atmosphere.

While traveling, Haafner divided his attention equally between nature and culture. He visited old temples and other shrines and sanctuaries, often ruins, and depicted them himself. Both in his love of the pluriform culture of the people and in his fascination with nature and ancient history, he appears to us as a true romantic.

In addition to the people, the landscape and nature of India evoked vehement emotions in Haafner. In his *Travels in a Palanquin* [*Reize in eenen Palanquin*] his description of Indian nature is almost religious in fervor and emotion, with the literary description of an overwhelming sunrise serving as a climax. It reads as a Romantic ode to the sun and to nature: how insignificant and trivial human life is compared to nature's majesty.

Another strong point of Haafner as a writer is his sense of humor. He might idealize the Indians and the Indian society, but his sense of humor guaranteed that he never went too far in this. He had a good feel for the bizarre and grotesque, and he described people and events with a sense of irony. His language is expressive and evocative, his style is the unparalleled result of a mixture of common sense and melodrama, and his favorite trope is hyperbole. His world is populated with odd characters who constantly run into the most peculiar situations. That must undoubtedly be the reason that Haafner's travel writing has sometimes been considered to be pure fantasy.

Fifty years ago Percy Adams wrote a small but influential book, *Travelers and Travel Liars 1600–1800*, that is still a classic treatment of travel writing as a literary and historic genre. This book discusses the historical reliability of the travelogue and discerns three categories. The first is that of the true travel story, written by a traveler who has visited the places he describes. The second is that of the imaginative travelogue, in which an author brings us to an invented world, e.g. Jonathan Swift's *Gulliver's Travels*. The third type is that of the armchair traveler: he is the travel liar, who describes a journey or a foreign country without ever having visited it personally. Instead of making a journey himself, he stays safely at home, consulting other travel writing and geographical descriptions and borrowing from them freely.

The market for travel writing in the seventeenth and eighteenth centuries was undoubtedly as great as it is today and many travelogues appeared that were wholly or partly invented, or copied from other ones. Often artists added illustrations to the travel writing that were artificial and showed only what Asia looked like in the imagination of the artist himself.

In Haafner's case it is quite clear that he was anything but an armchair traveler. Archival research conducted at the time of the preparation of the new edition of Haafner's works at the end of the last century verified much of what Haafner wrote about his life, the ships he was on, the places he lived, the jobs he had, and the friends that he made along the way. This research confirmed much of what he tells in his stories. Documents of the National Archives in The Hague, but also the India Office Library in London and the Sri Lankan archives in Colombo, show that all, or nearly all, the people he described, did in fact live in Asia and that they indeed held the jobs he attributed to them. Research successfully reconstructed his career as a VOC servant, among the items of proof turned up was a receipt of the monthly rent for his house in Calcutta where he lived as a free burgher.

In other respects, however, his work is certainly more literary, and closely follows the conventions and themes of his time. So we might conclude that Haafner described his own life and experiences with a certain accuracy, but that he did not hesitate, like many other writers, to borrow themes and stories from other books without mentioning his sources.

As a writer, Haafner idolized India and its inhabitants. But this qualification doesn't really do him justice: despite his fervent fascination with India he nevertheless remained an independent and critical observer with an open mind and observant eye for the ridiculous aspects of life in that country.

REIZE NAAR BENGALEN

EN

TERUGREIZE NAAR EUROPA

VAN

JACOB HAAFNER;

VOLGENS DESZELFS NAGELATENE PAPIEREN
UITGEGEVEN DOOR

C. M. HAAFNER.

MET PLATEN.

Te AMSTERDAM, bij
JOHANNES VAN DER HEY.
MDCCCXXII.

Fig. 3   Title page of *Reize naar Bengalen en terugreize naar Europa*
(Amsterdam 1822).

The mumbo-jumbo of all kinds of priests, religious functionaries, ascetics, and other denouncers of worldly matters, who tried to shake money out of the peoples' pockets through mysterious and obscure ceremonies, made him laugh. He tended to dislike the servants of the Almighty, whether they were Hindu, Catholic, or Protestant.

That became obvious in 1807, when he published a treatise which caused consternation in ecclesiastical circles in the Netherlands. Illustrative of Haafner's thinking and reflective of the books he was studying and reading during his years in Amsterdam, it is called *Onderzoek naar het nut der zendelingen en zendelings-genootschappen* [*Examination of the Usefulness of Missionaries and Missionary Societies*]. This was Haafner's submission for the essay contest organized by one of the oldest Dutch scholarly societies, Teylers Godgeleerd Genootschap (Teylers Theological Society) in Haarlem. The Society had asked for essays answering the question: what has been the use of missionary work in the overseas world in the past and what could possibly be done to improve this work in the future?

Who could have been better equipped to answer the question than Jacob Haafner? In barely 100 pages he made mincemeat of the missionaries. According to him the world has never seen a more criminal and hypocritical group of people than European missionaries. He points to all kinds of crimes and misbehavior, quotes extensively from other authors who were just as critical on Christianity and the missions, such as Voltaire, and has only one good piece of advice for the future: if anywhere in Asia one particular group of people needs the beneficial effects of the Gospel, it certainly is the Europeans themselves, and them alone.

But he issues a warning to the Society: if it were ever to send missionaries to evangelize the Europeans in Asia, these men should be fearless, because they would live in constant peril and fear of death. Haafner won the prize in 1805, but it took the cautious gentlemen of the Society two years before they had the book published in the prestigious *Transactions* series.

Reactions to Haafner

Haafner's way of thinking shocked his contemporaries. This can best be illustrated by the reactions to Haafner's treatise. This work, which can be viewed as his intellectual testament, was the topic of heated debates in missionary circles in the Netherlands, and essays were written to refute his assertions. By affirming other civilizations and putting them on equal footing with Christianity, rather than putting Western civilization first, Haafner's ideas were utterly unacceptable to his contemporaries. When Haafner praised the Vedas as an original Hindu work, for instance, one of his critics stated that they had surely been borrowed from the Christian Scriptures. The critic maintained that the Vedas were a corruption of the Holy Scriptures, and that it was time to re-introduce the *real* Vedas, as this was what the Hindus were waiting for. It was difficult indeed for many of Haafner's contemporaries to appreciate or even understand the multicultural perspective of this original and profound thinker.

This started to change with the publication of Haafner's travel writing. The publisher Adriaan Loosjes, who was on the board of the Teylers Theological Society, encouraged Haafner to write about his experiences in Asia. In 1806 his first travel writing appeared and became a bestseller. On the strength of this, Haafner was able to make a living from his writings for the rest of his life—which turned out to be unhappily short, as he died just three years later.

Readers were quick to appreciate the charms of Haafner's stories. This is the opening sentence of the very first review of Haafner's *Adventures on a Trip from Madras via Tranquebar to the Isle of Ceylon*, published in the authoritative literary periodical *Algemeene Vaderlandsche Letteroefeningen* [*General National Literary Exercises*] in 1807:

> These are no fabrications but real happenings and are links in a
> long chain of strange and bizarre adventures.

The reviewer praises Haafner's open attitude toward his fellow men and his abhorrence of tyranny, English imperialism in particular. The reviewer describes Haafner's literary style as lively, passionate, and moving. He is convinced that *Adventures* will be appreciated by its Dutch readership.

Haafner's writing spread from the Netherlands to the rest of Europe. His story about Mamia inspired Gaetano Gioja's ballet *I riti Indiani* (1814), the tale of a Dutchman who falls in love with an Indian temple dancer. The chapter about the *devadasis* in *Travels in a Palanquin* was the chief source of information for the French critics, among them Théophile Gautier, who reviewed the first performance of Indian *bayadères* in Paris in 1838. In that year, temple dancers from Thiruvanthipuram put on a series of performances in the Théâtre des Variétés in Paris and the Tivoli and Adelphi Theatres in London. Under the influence of Haafner, both the English and French critics wrote positive reviews of their performances, although they failed to grasp the deeper meaning conveyed by what was to their eyes an exotic dance. Nevertheless, they placed them in the same category as that of the then famous ballerina Maria Taglioni, who starred in Daniel Auber's ballet *Le Dieu et la Bayadère* (1830,

The God and the Bayadère). The *bayadères* became overnight celebrities who were depicted in popular magazines, and lithographs of them found a ready sale.

Haafner continued to find select readers. In 1867 another free-thinker, Multatuli, with whom Haafner has frequently been compared—unjustly because Multatuli was an advocate of the colonial expansion in the Dutch Indies—wrote of a recently published anthology:

> With only a few exceptions—I am thinking of the illiterate Haafner—nothing in it is worth reading.

Multatuli was obviously unaware of Haafner's multilingual talents and wide reading. It is no exaggeration to say that Haafner really stood out like a flaming beacon in the nineteenth-century Dutch literary landscape of the Netherlands.

The historical value of Haafner's writings became apparent in the twentieth century. The Sanskrit scholar Jean Philippe Vogel praised Haafner as the first Dutchman to have shown an unadulterated interest in the ideas of the Indians and stressed that Haafner's travel writing, though romantic, is an important source for our knowledge of Dutch commerce on the coasts of Bengal and Coromandel at the end of the eighteenth century. In another article Vogel praises Haafner for his accurate description of the temple complex of Mahabalipuram. According to Vogel it is the first academic description of these monuments in Western literature.

By the 1920s, Haafner found yet another appreciative audience, among the English-language readers in Ceylon. In the circle of the Dutch Burgher Union of Ceylon, which was founded in 1908, there was a vivid interest in Haafner's works. Two influential members of that Union, L.A. Prins and James Reginald Toussaint, started working on a new translation of his *Travels on Foot through the Island of Ceylon*. It was published as supplements to the *Journal of the Dutch Burgher Union of Ceylon* (1926–27). Anti-English remarks which were censored in the 1820s London translation are reintroduced in this edition. A comparison between both translations makes that blatantly clear.

The London translation leaves out the first paragraph and starts as follows:

> Having been prisoner-of-war for a considerable time in the city of Madras, I found it impossible to remain any longer a witness to the misery that prevailed in it, and in the being in great danger of also perishing in the general famine, I resolved to make my escape to the Danish settlement of Tranquebar, where I soon arrived in an open leaky boat.

The opening lines of the Colombo translation are quite different:

> A frightfully destructive war waged between the English and the Nabob of Mysore, Hyder Ali Chan, laid waste for almost three years the unhappy Carnactic and South Coromandel. The whole land was a scene of death and terror, and thousands of unfortunate natives of these once-flourishing and populous districts lost their lives by the sword or by the still more dreadful famine. Madras, the headquarters of the English, was in a pitiful and miserable condition. Continuously and for more than a year the city seemed as if it were covered by the bodies of dead and dying Indians. For a considerable time I was prisoner of war in this unfortunate city.

The translation of Prins and Toussaint must be seen against the background of the struggle for independence in Ceylon. By setting up Dutch language courses, the Dutch burghers tried to strengthen their identity; but due to lack of students and support from the "motherland", nothing came of it. The same went for Prins's and Toussiant's plans to translate more of Haafner's books.

An even more unlikely revival of Haafner's work occurred during the Second World War, when the anti-English character of Haafner's works were used in the propaganda effort of the National Socialist movement in the Netherlands. Shortly after the German invasion of that country, in 1940, a retranslation was published of *Adventures on a Trip from Madras via Tranquebar to the Isle of Ceylon* under the florid title of *Robbery and Destruction of our Colonies where Love and Prosperity Flourished*. Haafner's text was modernized, but nothing had to be added to highlight the perfidity of Great Britain. On the cover of the retranslation is written:

> For the past two centuries until the present day many of our German friends have contributed to the many-faceted work of colonization of our East Indies colonies, which has once more confirmed the ties of friendship between our two countries.

The publisher E.A.P. Dzur accentuates the wicked character of the English by stating that:

> Great Britain has consciously tried to cover up these evil deeds. Its representatives talk about humanity in order to cover up its own evil deeds. May this work of Haafner, and many more still unknown books, be published to enable the reader to come to the right conclusion.

A German translation of the aforementioned book was published under the title *A Journey from Madras to Ceylon: British Robbery and Devastation of Dutch Colonies* in 1941, and in 1943 a second impression appeared with the less propagandistic subtitle *Adventure on Land and at Sea*. Haafner escaped the classification of being a National Socialist writer, but someone lacking historical knowledge might easily place him in that category.

In the period after the Second World War, interest in Haafner's books waned in the Netherlands, which was also caused by the diminishing interest in the world behind the horizon after decolonization. It is also possible that Haafner was tainted by the National Socialist reprints which came out during the war.

A second revival of Haafner occurred after the republication of his complete works and the publication of his biography in Dutch at the beginning of this century. Interest in Haafner's work has undeniably grown over the past 30 years, not least because of his cosmopolitan, intercultural, and inclusive attitude which is revealed in his appreciation of other cultures and his unsurpassed ability to identify with the other. This kind of attitude is less suited to the style of politicians and preachers of penitence who thrived and thrive on societal contradictions. Haafner stresses the many similarities, both positive and negative, which exist between peoples and cultures on this planet. He formulated his point of departure, which was derived from the French Revolution, very succinctly:

> I deem all people, no matter what the color of their skin, or to
> what nation they belong or to which religion they adhere, to be
> my fellow-human being and brother.

This creed, which tends to be paid lip-service rather than recruit true followers, was Haafner's life mission; now Haafner may find an audience who truly seeks to understand him.

My Journey to Haafner

Thirty years ago my journey to Jacob Haafner began by chance. A businessman from India with a company in Amsterdam asked me what was written in the seventeenth and eighteenth centuries about India in the Netherlands. He hoped that I would discover material on which a movie could be based. After a few months I gave him a summary of the limited literature on India in the Dutch language with the advice to use the book *Travels in a Palanquin* by a certain Jacob Haafner. On the basis of that book a script was written in

Bangalore with the title *The Emerald Route*. The manuscript was rejected and this seemed to be the end of a promising project.

But I had been put on the track of Haafner and wanted to know more about him. For me Haafner was a real discovery primarily as a radical thinker about relations with the non-Western world, but also as a writer. How was it possible that someone who wrote such readable and humorous prose could be completely forgotten?

The idea took shape slowly to republish his works, but I was apprehensive about the magnitude of the task. I was lucky to find an ally in my colleague Jaap de Moor. We worked in the late eighties and early nineties at the Instituut voor de Geschiedenis van de Europese Expansie en Reacties daarop (IGEER) (Institute for the History of European Expansion and Reactions Thereupon) at Leiden University. We drew up a plan for the republication of his works and were able to convince the Linschoten Vereeniging to publish his travelogues in their illustrious series *Werken* [*Works*]. After we collected enough pledges for grants, the board of the Association gave its blessing to an annotated reissue in three volumes of the *Works of Jacob Haafner*.

For almost five years we undertook research in our spare time in the National Archives in The Hague, which revealed that Haafner had largely based his stories on verifiable facts and events. I also visited in those years places that were associated with Haafner's life and undertook research in archives in Colmar, Haafner's birthplace, Halle an der Saale, the India Office Library in London, and the National Archives in Colombo. We published a number of articles in academic journals.

The launch in 1993 of the first volume took place in the Letterkundig Museum (Museum for Literature) in The Hague, where at the same time also an exhibition "Nederlanders over Azië 1770–1830" ("Dutch on Asia 1770–1830") was being held. Serving as a catalog for this exhibition was an illustrated book entitled *Uit Menschlievendheid zoude ik barbaar kunnen worden. Reizen in Azië 1770–1830* [*My Love of Humankind Could Turn Me into a Barbarian. Travels in Asia 1770–1830*]. Publication of the first volume of Haafner's writings (the other two volumes appeared in 1995 and 1997 respectively) was followed by a series of positive reviews in the press. Encouraged by this, Jaap and I became a double act, giving lectures and trekking around the country. We were known as the "Haafner brothers" because we propagated Haafner and his ideas with what some considered almost missionary zeal.

Together with Kees Slager of the radio program Onvoltooid Verleden Tijd (OVT) [Imperfect Past Tense] we compiled a series about the decline of the VOC under the title "De Doorluchtige Compagnie" ["The Illustrious

Company"]. One episode was dedicated to Haafner's stay in India and his anti-colonial ideas. All these activities led to the first volume of writings being sold out in a short time. When the final volume was published, we re-issued the first volume, and the collected works were published as a trilogy.

Through this republication, Haafner regained some prominence amongst lovers of travel writing, colonial historians, and scholars who use travelogues for research. In this re-issue, Haafner's nineteenth-century Dutch was followed, given the academic premise of the series. The use of that Dutch does not detract from the legibility, but it may still have constituted too high a threshold for the average reader. In addition the beautifully executed works are not exactly cheap.

For me, this was a reason to think about how Haafner could reach the even wider audience which I felt he deserved. After I had completed my PhD thesis in 2000, I launched a website and devoted a section to Haafner (www.paulvandervelde.nl/haafner). It contains overviews of all his publications, publications about him, and reviews. Encouraged by the number of visitors to the website, the idea of writing a popular biography of Haafner took shape. After I had obtained the support of the Dutch Foundation for Literature and the Dutch Fund for In-depth Journalism, the work began in late 2002. The publisher Bert Bakker had already declared its willingness to publish my book.

This led to a further expanding of the Haafner research and the organization of a workshop on his 250th birthday at the Frankesche Stiftungen in his hometown of Halle in 2004. The results of the research of the participants have been included in this biography. There was also an exhibition in the India Hall of the Stiftungen, where virtually all versions of Haafner's books and engravings were shown.

In early 2006 Haafner was included in the Digital Library of Dutch Literature, reflecting his new status in the pantheon of Dutch literature. In the biography I chose to render extracts from Haafner's work in a more modern way, while trying as much as possible to follow his style. For the choice of extracts, I sought out his more informal images of India, expressed in encounters with people of all types and humorous descriptions of society and nature, usually missing from contemporary European writing of that world.

I see this biography as the completion of a project which I started in 1987, which has brought me into contact with Haafner brothers and sisters from across the world and has led me to places where Haafner found his inspiration. These encounters and experiences have played a major role in comprehending Haafner's sublime world. What remains is the quest for translations into other languages—his entire oeuvre has in recent years been translated into the modern German—and putting a plaque on his final residence, the house De Drie Bloeyende Koornaaren (The Three Flowering Wheat Ears) in Amsterdam, where he died in 1809.

I wrote this book in Amsterdam, like Haafner, with the same longing for the tropics. The big difference was that I was able to satisfy my desire by regularly escaping the cloudy gray sky of Amsterdam. This, and also the discovery of three original manuscripts of Haafner in 2006 which offer a different look on his career as a writer, are the reasons why the completion of the biography took longer than I had initially anticipated.

It took longer still for this English translation to appear. I did not do it; but about two years ago, Liesbeth Bennink contacted me in relation to an image of a Dutch trader on an Indian temple: "Could it be Haafner?" It was not Haafner and it took Liesbeth less than a year to translate my Haafner biography. Liesbeth certainly is one of Haafner's reincarnations. She has lived in India for 25 years and had a relationship with a Brahmin, so she is conversant with the Indian way of life which shines through in her wonderful translation from the Dutch original. I am the only person to blame for things which were lost in the crossing.

Paul van der Velde
Amsterdam, 1 July 2020

Chapter 1

A Wandering Existence

Before the fall of the Berlin Wall, Halle on the Saale was a gray industrial town with blocks of houses lined up like a nightmare from Kafka. The old city centre, dominated by the steeples of the Liebfrauenkirche, was completely dilapidated. Trams narrowly passed by the statue of the George Friedrich Handel, born here in 1685, standing patiently on his pedestal in the middle of the marketplace. At the beginning of the twenty-first century the city makes a much more lively impression. The old town centre is busily being restored. The emissions of the chemical plants in the area have been greatly reduced, and Handel looks fresh again. Despite these efforts, the city is suffering from the shrinking cities syndrome: more than 100,000 people have left since the end of the Cold War.

Halle's heyday was in the eighteenth century, when it was the center of Pietism, a Protestant movement which stressed missionary activities. The Franckesche Stiftungen [Francke Foundations] founded by August Hermann Francke were the focal point of this. Halle's university, now the Martin Luther University of Halle-Wittenberg, had an excellent reputation in the eighteenth century, especially in the area of the study of theology and medicine. Jacob Haafner's father Matthias Haafner arrived at the university around 1750.

Matthias Haafner hailed from the picturesque city of Colmar in the Alsace. (Anyone opening the phonebook there today will still come across pages full of Haffners.) Jean Jacques Haffner, Jacob's grandfather, had been counselor of the city around the middle of the eighteenth century. The Catholic Haffners belonged to the administrative elite of Colmar. Louis XIV awarded Jacob's grandfather a coat of arms for the many services he had rendered. For Jacob's father, Matthias, born in 1723 and the eldest son in this Catholic family, a career in the clergy was an obvious choice. He was sent to a nearby monastery where he took the vow after a year's novitiate.

> [My father] forced himself to satisfy the wishes of his parents for
> some time, but soon started to resent the fasting, vigils, praying,
> and singing so much that he decided to escape. He could not
> see himself having to spend his whole life in the monotony of
> a monastery.

Jacob later recorded the story of this escape which had been related to him
by an acquaintance of his father whom he met in India. That Matthias sought
refuge in Germany is hardly surprising. Alsace was then as it is now a melting
pot of French and German culture, and it is highly likely that Matthias was
bilingual in French and German. Many French names turn up in the office of
the land registry in Halle, where they were listed as students.

Haafner's grandparents resigned themselves to the decision of their son
to study medicine in Halle, especially after he took up residence with their
distant acquaintances, the Happach family, who belonged to Halle's middle
class. In 1695, Martin Happach had become a citizen of the city, where he
practiced the trade of boot and saddle maker. Apparently he did well: in 1744
he was the proprietor of two large adjacent buildings, numbers 20–22 on the
Grosse Ulrichstrasse, then and now the main thoroughfare of Halle. In these
buildings his leather goods store was situated.

After some time Matthias began a relationship with the daughter of the
family, Sophia. When he informed his parents that he wanted to marry her,
they were not amused. The Happachs were acquaintances, but Lutheran and
of a lower social stratum. Matthias's parents informed Matthias that they
would disinherit him if he persisted. Undoubtedly the Haffners tried to
convince Sophia's parents of their view. Initially this had an effect, because
the Happachs declared themselves against the marriage.

Carefree

Sophia Happach and Matthias Haafner could not be dissuaded from their
intention. According to Jacob, they made up a ruse:

> Sophia told her mother that she had already involved herself
> with my father to such an extent that she could not show herself
> in public, except as his wife. After the first storm had subsided,
> her parents consented in the marriage on the condition that
> Matthias would convert to Lutheranism. He had no problem
> with that because he had been planning already to rid of himself
> from the shackles with which the Roman Catholic faith binds
> the mind and heart of its faithful.

He continued: "In the year 1755, the 13th of May, I came into the world at Halle."

On closer inspection, this turns out to be a second ruse, a fib to cover up his parents' naughtiness. His parents had been married on October 21, 1753; less than seven months later, on May 13, 1754, Jacob was born in one of the two houses belonging to the Happachs. For a long time Haafner was able to hoodwink everyone, but when the archives in Halle became freely accessible again after the fall of the Berlin Wall, the truth came to light: Jacob Haafner was a year older than he pretended. But in almost all publications on Haafner the wrong year of birth—1755—is given. His sister Sophia was born in Emden that year, where the newly-graduated doctor Matthias had moved shortly after the birth of Jacob.

"Thus my wandering life started early," Jacob wrote, somewhat more truthfully.

His father's practice would not flourish. Probably on the advice of Jacob's godfather, Jacob Tegel—the director of the Brandenburg East India Company, who had also made a career in the VOC (Vereenigde Oostindische Compagnie, the Dutch East India Company), because of which he had ample means—Matthias Haafner became a ship's doctor. The Emden Company, based in the Baltic port of that name, owned a trading post in the Chinese city of Canton (present-day Guangzhou). Haafner claimed that his father made a trip to China from 1757 to 1760 as a ship's doctor, but no ship of that Company sailed to Canton in the period that the Haafner family lived in Emden. We do know from sources in the municipal archive of Emden that Matthias was the founder of St. Johannis Pax et Concordia, a Masonic lodge. Little is known of the activities of this lodge but membership of Freemasonry was a signature of the liberal bourgeois milieu in which Haafner grew up. Founded in 1763, it was in contact with Freemasons in Berlin according to a brochure on the occasion of its 250th anniversary. Much of the Emden archive was lost during the Second World War, so nothing is known about Haafner's childhood in that city. In the preserved church book of the Evangelical Lutheran parish of Emden, the birth of Haafner's brother, Christian Matthias, was recorded in 1761.

Late in 1765, the family emerges in Amsterdam, a city, at that time, of 220,000 inhabitants. The Haffners were not the first and certainly not the last Germans seeking better opportunities in cosmopolitan Amsterdam. There was a large German community, and the Haffners registered with the Lutheran church. This is all that is known from the sources about the first 12 years of Haafner's life. Everything else we know about his childhood is derived from his own writings. From these, it can be deduced that he received primary education in Emden and Amsterdam. He learned arithmetic, German, and Dutch. The rest of his education he got from his father who taught him High German (which Haafner calls his mother tongue), French, and Latin.

Jacob certainly did not have a low opinion of his own intellectual faculties. He had an astonishing memory and easily absorbed everything. He lived after his father's maxim that what somebody else could learn, he could also master. He prided himself on this characteristic: it came in handy many times in his life. According to his own testimony, he overcame difficulties that discouraged others, such as when he had to teach himself bookkeeping and English in a very short time. The latter he did (according to his own statement) in six months. It is true that Jacob was not academically trained, but the education that he did receive gave him a great advantage over most of his contemporaries, who could hardly read, write, or calculate. His flair for languages was later of great advantage to him in the polyglot world of the Indian subcontinent.

Jacob felt his childhood was far too brief. He looks back on his childhood with an overwhelming feeling of nostalgia, a trope which would become popular in novels at the end of the nineteenth century:

> Happy time of childhood, of innocence and joy. How pleasant is it to bring back to my mind that bygone era and to transpose myself into all the little details of that carefree time. Too soon you passed by! In those years people experience innocent pleasures that make the bitter setbacks of later age bearable. But before I realized, I had fallen prey to a wandering and needy existence far from my family, at the mercy of the capricious and barbaric treatment of rough and ruthless persons.

Jacob's "wandering and needy" life started when his father entered the service of the VOC. He decided to take his eldest son on the journey. In Amsterdam Matthias had failed to find employment as a doctor. Jacob gives an interpretation why that was the case, an interpretation that is at the same time a reflection of his own social position when he was writing his travel stories:

> He was a stranger without friends, without sponsorship, and the object of envy and opposition of his colleagues. He soon found that skill and competence alone are not enough to succeed.

Ship's doctors were in great demand, especially if experienced. With 36 guilders per month it was one of the best paid jobs on board. Jacob, who enrolled in the lowest rank of "boy", had to manage with five guilders, but he was allowed to sleep with his father in a cabin. By taking Jacob with him, Matthias relieved

Fig. 4 Medallion of Jacob Haafner. Oil on canvas, approx. 1766. Private collection.

his wife, who was entrusted with the care of Jacob's brother and sister. With the advance he took on his wages, she could certainly manage for a year.

First Adventure in Porto Praya

On June 25, 1766, Jacob, who had just turned 12, departed with his father on the ship *Luxemburg* to the East. It had slightly more than 300 crew on board and stood under the command of skipper Claas Roem. Much has been written about life on board the VOC ships. The crew was densely packed together, which guaranteed friction. Often there were outbreaks of infectious diseases, and sanitary conditions were horrible. This resulted in an average death rate of 10 per cent of the crew. Weather conditions, from week-long doldrums to terrifying storms, contributed to already existing tensions on the ship. Headwinds also affected the *Luxemburg*, which only reached the harbor of the refreshment station Porto Praya in the Cape Verde islands, a Portuguese colony, after two months. Here Jacob was first introduced to the world that would so much determine his life. He also experienced a frightening adventure.

He accompanied his father when he went to make a visit to the Portuguese governor.

> The Governor lives in a kind of fortress on a steep mountain near the sea. As is common to children, I walked through all the rooms of the building and saw several black women busy with the pilling of cotton or something like that. I wanted to leave, but they took me by the hand and made me sit down beside them. They gave me lots of fruits and sweets on which I feasted. Then one of the women, who had left for a short while, conveyed to me that my father was looking for me and that she had been asked to take me back to him. This was true, but they had deceived him and said that I had walked down the hill on the way to the well where our people were busy filling barrels.
>
> It started getting dark and I followed the woman outside. Shortly thereafter we were joined by a negro to whom she entrusted me. She made it clear by signs that he would take me to my father who was waiting for me in a house. When I passed a big building, I saw severed heads that had been put on stakes in front of it. I was terribly shocked and looked anxiously around to see if I could flee. Eventually I was brought into a house. There was a man who had the appearance of a priest, and he told me in broken Latin I need not fear. I nonetheless became

very anxious and asked emphatically where my father was. They tried to reassure me, and I was given all kinds of delicacies to keep me quiet. In the meantime it had already become quite dark. I became more and more frightened because I was not used to seeing black people. My fear increased because the priest and the man who had brought me were whispering in the corner of the room where they occasionally, I thought, looked at me sideways.

Suddenly I got up from my seat with a random movement, ran quickly across the room, pulled open the nearest door, and with one jump I was outside. The black woman who had brought me from the Governor's Mansion, who I thought had left already, stood at the door and tried to stop me. Luckily I managed to get away from her and ran on the road at full speed without knowing where I was going or looking to see if they were chasing me or not. I was already exhausted when I finally saw two of our crew members on donkeys. They had been sent to look for me. I told them what had happened, but no one could understand why the black jokers had tried to keep me with them. Possibly they wanted to take me in the night to Santiago, the capital of the island, which is only a few miles from Porto Praya, to make of me what they wished, me being still young. Possibly their goal was only to entertain themselves with me and my anxiety. In any event, I was happy, and my father no less, that the thought of escape had occurred to me at the right time. A few days after we weighed anchor, abundantly supplied with fresh water, cattle, birds, fruits, and other products of the island.

The latter was just as well because, as previously noted, the rest of the journey did not go smoothly. The descriptions of life on board given by Haafner are acute and humorous at the same time:

The wind which had been unfavorable since our departure from Europe, became even more adverse. Quickly a scene of human misery unfolded aboard, of which only seafarers can have an adequate idea. Because many had eaten themselves to sickness with all kinds of fruits at Santiago, almost all got dysentery. Shortly after, infectious fevers broke out, which are almost always fatal near the equator, where we had lain already for three weeks without advancing a mile. Not a day passed without one of the victims being entrusted to the ocean. We lay there in the most suffocating heat for three terrible long weeks as if nailed on a flat endless water pond. The burning sunbeams that shone from a clear cloudless sky with a deadly silence straight down on our heads chased everyone from the deck. An oppressive smell of sickness and the groans of the sick made dwelling in the steerage equally intolerable.

Matthias Haafner became infected as well, and Jacob feared for his father's life. He took courage when the signal came that the Cape of Good Hope was in sight.

The Cape of Good Hope

Shortly thereafter we saw land. The Cape of Good Hope! The activity and the noise on the deck caused by this news so enjoyable by all was noticed by my father. I told him what it meant. He told me that he wanted to go ashore. Alas! His desire was fulfilled, but only to be buried there.

The ship's log of the *Luxemburg* states that Matthias Haffner died on December 7, 1766 without leaving a will. He left some goods which were auctioned off. He was one of the 28 crew members who did not survive the journey. Jacob was desperate: what was to become of him?

At the time about 20 thousand people lived in the Cape colony, of which 6,500 in Cape Town. There were 1,600 VOC officials and military personnel and the rest consisted of free citizens with their families and slaves from Indonesia and Madagascar. On the land around the Cape lived the Khoikhoi (called *Hottentotten* by the Dutch). Cape Town had been founded in 1652 by Jan van Riebeeck. In a century, Cape Town had developed into a well-equipped refreshment station where all the ships on the way to the East docked. It was of great strategic importance and had strong fortifications and a large military garrison.

A VOC bookkeeper from Halle, who knew the Happachs, took pity on Jacob. He temporarily went to live outside town with his family when a smallpox epidemic broke out in May 1767. Jacob was not infected, but later that year he contracted "putrid fever" or typhoid and was admitted to the hospital, according to the Cape daily logs.

Shortly after his discharge he witnessed the execution of a young slave girl who was accused of arson. Slavery was a source of unprecedented social tension in Cape Town. Slaves were regularly racked, burned alive, or publicly executed in other horrible ways. The execution made a deep impression on Jacob:

> The girl I saw burned alive was a young slave of Chrispijn, a Cape citizen. She was accused of having intended to set her master's house on fire. O! I will never forget the groaning of the pitiable, and how, when the flames licked her face, she tore the cloth from her neck to cover her face with it.

In the daily log of Cape Town, in which the VOC officials registered all kinds of events, there is a brief mention of it: "Saturday September 24th, the slave Clarinde of Batavia, the arsonist, is strapped on a pole with an iron bracket and held upright and standing with a chain, further by the wood, stacked around and fired, burnt alive to ashes." It was a small taste of what waited for him in Batavia (now known as Jakarta). With a recommendation in his pocket to work there as a clerk in the VOC office, he sailed on November 19, 1767 on the *Leimuiden*.

Adultery and Torture

Around his arrival in early 1768, Batavia had already lost much of the seventeenth-century luster which had made it known as the "pearl of the East". It was still, however, a very lively trading center and the capital of the Dutch colonial possessions in Asia. Jacob was hired by the chief merchant Robbert van der Burg as a private tutor to teach his two children decent Dutch. Jacob lived with the family and came to know the dark sides of a slave society in the environment of a private household.

He started his assignment in an upbeat mood. The children demanded all his attention and he had, to his great regret, no time left for other things. He was bored of doing nothing but tutoring. Jacob wanted to leave but van der Burg made little effort to find work for him at the VOC office because the children had become attached to their tutor. Coincidence helped him a bit. Just after Jacob left for a trip with the children and van der Burg, the latter asked him to return home to pick up a book which he had forgotten.

It was in his wife's room. Innocently Jacob stepped into her room:

> When I opened the door I saw Madame in an unmistakably unambiguous position on the sofa with the music master Vonk. I stood transfixed in the doorway and could not speak a word. At first they were as stunned as I, but because she probably

thought me too young to understand what they were doing, Madame gave me the book without any embarrassment.

Having surprised his boss, she did everything she could to get rid of the witness. She got her way eventually. But it was some of her other practices which were even more distressing to Haafner:

Mrs. V.d.B. was an evil bitch who took a barbarous pleasure in severely punishing her house slaves at the slightest "offense" and in being personally present at the punishment. It was her favorite pastime to make up the accounts, as she herself called it, on Friday evenings so they could be settled the next day. She held session each Saturday because she always managed in one week to uncover many violations, each more ridiculous than the next. There were always plenty of slaves she could pass sentence on. In one word, she played executioner. It was her weakness and, apart from the music lessons with Vonk, her only pleasure, the good soul!

Very early Saturday morning the house echoed with the lamentations of the poor slaves, fearing from the disgruntled glances of their executioner in the past week, that soon the split reed would rip apart their skin. Yes, reader! This tigress had the cane which she used for her punishments split into four, so that, when it descended on the naked bodies of the poor creatures, it gripped and tore the skin.

No court could ever be accused of being more punctual in its execution of punishment than Mrs. V.d.B. One after the next, each "criminal" was bound upright to a ladder and punished. She watched cold-blooded as her victims coiled under the most wrenching pains and counted the clattering blows with a pompousness which would have made a real magistrate jealous. Nothing was more annoying and offensive at the same time.

When, as often happened in this house and was definitely not unusual, a slave was forced to flog until bleeding his own wife, perhaps the mother of his children, or heard her screaming in her pregnant state for mercy under his blows, whose mind is not filled with horror? Who can blame these people of warlike and "vindictive" nature or be surprised that when they are finally seized by anger and despair and, having numbed their senses by the use of hefty amounts of opium, decide to liberate themselves from their suffering by their suicide, after first

LOTGEVALLEN

EN

VROEGERE ZEEREIZEN

VAN

JACOB HAAFNER;

VOLGENS DESZELFS NAGELATENE PAPIEREN
UITGEGEVEN DOOR

C. M. HAAFNER.

MET PLATEN.

Bl. 72.

Te AMSTERDAM, bij
JOHANNES VAN DER HEY.
MDCCCXX.

Fig. 5   Title page of *Lotgevallen en vroegere zeereizen van Jacob Haafner* (Amsterdam 1820).

cooling their rightful vengeance on their white oppressors, or anything in their path?

Jacob was fed up with the colonial world and embarked on the *Jerusalem* with the intention to return to Amsterdam. He didn't reach any further than Cape Town because his wages booklet, necessary for the passage to the Netherlands had been left in Batavia. He almost did not even reach Cape Town, because the ship sustained heavy damage in one of the many storms that Haafner would experience. Haafner's involuntary stay in South Africa would take more than a year, and reluctantly he had to accept a job with a slave keeper. Meanwhile, he occasionally had the time to enjoy nature, and he climbed the famous Table Mountain several times.

Khoikhoi Love Beads

The panorama that one enjoys on the Table Mountain is of exceptional beauty. You see the houses of the city as a few white spots and the bay with its vessels as a small water bowl with black dots. On the one side, the Dutch Hottentot mountains stretch away, and on the other side is an immense sea surface surrounded by a row of mountains and cliffs along which the surf appears as a silver lining. This is a rich reward for the effort of climbing and lets the viewer fall silent with elation.

Haafner's description of the Table Mountain cloud formation known as the "tablecloth" may be one of the first in Western literature:

Sometimes one can see whitish clouds floating towards the mountain at a high speed. Immense clouds pile up together against the sides of the mountain and come nearer and nearer. One feels overcome by arbitrary fear and surrounded in an instant by clouds which completely take away the view. This is the so-called tablecloth, the precursor of the violent south-eastern winds that descend on the plain and the city with furious violence or release themselves in rain. On the top of Table Mountain, one sees just a light breeze and damp fog amidst the clouds. Not long after the clouds descend, and one is again shone upon by the sun while in the plain heavy winds rage or torrential rains fall.

Jacob had also developed a fascination for plants and often went out there to look for rare species:

I had already collected some plants when coming to the other side of the mountain I saw a young Hottentot girl of exceptional beauty. She belonged to the few remaining independent Hottentot tribes that live at the outermost boundaries of the colony. They had come to the Cape to complain to the Government about the arbitrary behavior of the tyrannical Boers and to ask justice for their glaring suffering.

It seemed as though she had seated herself there to enjoy the vastness and to view the flag that had just announced the vicinity of a ship at sea.

When she became aware of me and saw what I was doing, she got up and helped me search. When I had collected a sufficient amount, I sat down to rest, tired from the climbing and the heat. Without a trace of fear, she sat directly next to me. She took the cloth with which I wiped my sweaty torso from my hands and wiped it over my face with clear pleasure. Aside from the disgusting mixture of grease and soot with which she, like all other Hottentot, was covered and which did not do disadvantage to her figure, she was the most charming and most attractively shapely image that one can imagine of a woman. Instead of the flat nose—usually the characteristic of the Hottentot who suffer under oppression and slavery—she had a full countenance with very charming features, a row of shining white teeth and a fiery wide open eye. The well proportioned limbs and her shapely bosom made her one of the rare beauties in which nature had already collected all her art to compensate for the general ugliness of her nation.

I spoke to her in Dutch, which she didn't understand, and I did not understand the Hottentot language, in which she answered me. After we had tried to contact each other for some time through signs, I was getting ready to leave. She followed me to halfway down the mountain. There she stopped me and pointed out the camp of her tribe. She also made clear with signs she wanted to see me here again early the next morning. After a brief interval in which her earlier friskiness turned to sadness, she ran her hand over my face and then ran with incomprehensible speed down the mountain and soon disappeared behind the bushes.

I did not know what to think of this meeting. Captain Hanssen and his wife, to whom I told this story, laughed heartily, and wished me luck with my Hottentot conquest. Nevertheless, I went back to our meeting place the following morning. But how great was my disappointment. Khoikhoi, camp, everything was gone. They had left at the earliest dawn, as I heard afterwards. They were indignant that the Government had tried to satisfy them with empty promises and fine words as usual.

When I arrived at our meeting place, I found a row of beads that she wore around her arms, legs, and neck. She probably had put them there when she realized that she had to leave suddenly, with the intention that I would find and keep them. I took them with me in any case, and this was the only memento that I kept of my Hottentot sweetheart.

Haafner failed to understand that the beads formed a declaration of love for the Khoikhoi, a people that he knew as Hottentots. Shortly after his amorous adventure he received his wages book and on his sixteenth birthday he embarked on the ship *Lands Welvaren* under skipper Simon Bot and bade farewell to the Cape and its hospitable residents.

Famous Lost Son

On August 21, 1770, the ship arrived at the Texel harbor after a smooth trip. "Unaware of what was waiting for me and overwhelmed by soothing dreams there was no happier and more joyful creature than I, when after a successful trip the Dutch coast came into view." He went with a mate on a smaller ship to Amsterdam and at a stopover in Medemblik they pulled a prank on a lady innkeeper.

My friend and I went ashore where we asked an old woman where we could have a drink. The good old lady, realising we had just arrived from India, asked us how her son, who had gone to the East, but from whom she had heard nothing for five years, was doing. She described with exact precision his face, posture, and manners with the bias of a mother. She showed us also his birth and baptismal name which were written out in a church ledger. She had no doubt that we knew him. She lived under the impression that the Indies were as big as her small town and that everyone knew each other personally as they did in Medemblik.

To mock her a little, we told her that not only had we been very good friends with her son, but also that he was doing very well, and that he was on his way to make his fortune. He had no

Fig. 6 From *Lotgevallen en vroegere zeereizen* (Amsterdam 1820). Sixteen-year-old Jacob Haafner with a Khoikhoi girl on the slopes of the Table Mountain, South Africa.

doubt that he would soon come back to his mother laden with treasures. Upon hearing this exciting news, she cried on top of her voice to her daughter and maid with whom she shared the joyful news. Then she walked out of the door in flying hurry and returned not long afterwards. She was followed by a bunch of farmers, probably her neighbors, who overwhelmed us with questions about the famous progeny. Although our answers were often inconsistent with each other, they took no heed and their imaginations filled in what was lacking in our story.

Out of sheer joy, the good woman asked us into her best room and in one beat had laden the table with sandwiches, salmon, cake, brandy, coffee, and all that with which she thought to spoil us. We could have easily brought some friends along, although we did our best to help reduce her stock. Indeed, the treats were a godsend: for months we had eaten only salt beef, hard biscuits, peas, and rancid bacon. This food came as a boon, and the woman had certainly not invited us for nothing.

When it got dark and we had to go back on board, she sent us a supper with two bottles of wine and invited us to come for coffee the next day. In short, during the two days that we were forced to stay in Medemblik, she showered us with benefactions, and on our departure she provisioned us generously. She even wanted to give us three guilders, but we thought we should refuse, however much my friend afterwards regretted this "stupidity", as he called it. That this little deception of this family would be reprehensible, I dare not hesitate to answer in the negative. After all, we gave back to the poor woman and her friends the joy and pleasure for at least a few years, and brought them in a pleasant delusion that even might come true. By doing the opposite, we would only have unnecessarily increased their sadness, in which they were immersed for some time because of uncertainty about the fate of their beloved child who was, in all probability, already dead.

The Umbilical Cord Unravels

On August 21, 1770, Jacob arrived in Amsterdam and, after some days searching, found his mother in a slum in appalling conditions. Their reunion was emotional.

> She did not recognize me immediately, but the flood of tears that welled up in my eyes and my voice interrupted by sobs made her recognize me suddenly. With loud screaming she threw herself at me without being able to utter a word. Oh, with what emotion I felt my mother's tears rolling down my face. What a glorious feeling warmed my heart when I first consciously experienced her motherly caresses. No, all the delusions have nothing comparable with the pure emotion one feels when one is lying after a long absence at the throbbing chest of the source of one's life. Especially when this precious creature has been torn from its comfortable existence and has been thrown into extremely deep distress, and the heart is overcome at once by love, compassion, respect, and melancholy.

Jacob recounted the sad story of the death of Matthias and of the many adventures he had encountered in the course of three years. But where were his brother and sister? She told how she had been paid 103 guilders only at the beginning of the year at the East India House, half of what remained after the auction of her husband's belongings and his salary after deducting the advance. The other half had been given to a guardian who had been appointed by the city orphan masters. This governmental patronizing had been too much for her. She had returned to Halle with her children and had entrusted her son to Jacob Tegel, Jacob's godfather, who had placed him in the orphanage of the Franckesche Foundation in preparation for his studies in theology. His sister was entrusted to the care of Tegel's daughter, Sophia. After a quarrel with the Tegels she had returned to Amsterdam where she thought she could support herself with needlework. Jacob himself could see that she had not succeeded in this, and he blamed her condition on her own arrogance and vanity, because she would have much better stayed with her family in Halle.

She asked him how much he was owed by the VOC. Jacob reassured her and said they could expect to manage for some time with the 400 guilders he was expecting. When on August 29 he approached the cashier of the East India House, he was let down. Because of all kinds of deductions applied by the VOC, he received only half. It was still a significant amount. On the way home he came across the merchant J. Hilkes who was a member of the Lutheran diaconate. Hilkes managed to convince the young man that it was better to let him keep the money. He would use it to pay for Jacob's vocational training. The latter, perhaps looking for a father figure, was persuaded. His mother's disappointment was huge when he told her, and she seems to even have filed a lawsuit against her own son and Hilkes to get her hand on his wages.

Thus Jacob withdrew from the authority of his mother, who cursed him. Hilkes apprenticed him to a painter. It is likely that Jacob worked in the studio of the famous engraver Reinier Vinkeles, who would later convert many of Jacob's drawings into engravings for his travelogues. They are all included in this biography.

> I had been attracted to painting and drawing since my childhood. I covered all pieces of paper which came into my reach with drawings, and daubed all walls I came across. It was not hard to make a choice, and I informed my benefactor, which he truly was, about my love for art. He kept his word, and shortly afterwards he placed me with a famous painter.

He was one of the 13 students who worked at the studio. His activities consisted mainly of mixing paint and pumicing carriage panels. He made very good progress in painting and would have come far were it not that there was tension between him and the oldest student.

He was only partially happy in the boarding house of the parish clerk of the Lutheran church, where he was placed. The sexton had a 19-year-old daughter who fell in love with him. Jacob answered this love, because of his lack of experience, only just before he left. He first saw her as his guardian angel who saved him from the temptations of the city:

> I owe it to her that the efforts of my fellow pupils to drag me to the pubs and bring me to bad company were in vain, because she convinced me of its abhorrence, and therefore I spent my free time pleasantly and usefully in her presence. Furthermore, the boarding and lodging was downright bad. I had to sleep with three other orphans in a narrow bed under a thin blanket. The poor and bad living in this house had totally robbed me of any interest in this struggling existence and I decided, without further consulting with anyone, to say goodbye to the profession of painter and to try my luck again at sea.

When he departed on June 8, 1771 as an apprentice seaman on the *Bleijenburg* under skipper Cornelis Bos, he did not know he would never again see his mother alive. Admittedly he patched up the quarrel with his mother before he left, but his decision to leave her continued to haunt him until the end of his life.

I left my poor mother in a foreign country heavy-hearted, without friends or resources. She did not have the slightest prospect to wrestle herself from her miserable condition. Alas! When I look back I consider myself an ungrateful creature. I should have stayed with her and should have put up with the lowest and most degrading work, rather than leaving her, to whom I owed my life, to her miserable fate. God only knows how much remorse I have felt about that in my later life. But I was too young and reckless, and, as I said, life ashore was not to my liking. I was also already gripped by the wanderlust that made me unfit to lead a monotonous life in subordinate posts. He who is haunted by this evil spirit, constantly wants to go somewhere else and thinks he can find happiness only where he is not.

Haafner was clearly afflicted with *Sehnsucht* that would make him roam from one place to another for the next 15 years. He kept his family in the loop of his wanderings. This becomes clear from, amongst other places, the 1783 baptismal register of Norderney, an island off the northern coast of Germany, in which Haafner, in absentia, is registered as godfather of a child of his brother, the pastor on the island. It is written: "Jacob Haafner in Bengal". It would be another two years before he would set foot in India for the first time.

Chapter 2

Struggle for Life

Haafner's departure from Europe in 1771 was his second journey to the East. Haafner describes the details of these journeys but mainly pays attention to the more dramatic and human aspects. He says he has been in danger innumerable times while traveling at sea. This may sound like an exaggeration, but the storms he describes can all be found in the ships' logs, recorded there in a dry and matter-of-fact way. The *Bleijenburg* arrived on September 24, 1771 in Cape Town and left two weeks later. After spending three weeks in the French-occupied island of Réunion, they continued their journey across the Indian Ocean and ended up in a terrible storm. The ship almost sank because of the negligence of a French officer.

The Sleeping Sickness of Sardis

At the Cape we had taken a French naval officer named Sardis on board with whom our captain had arranged free passage to Batavia if he would keep watch along with the mates. This officer, who was a skilled sailor, had for his profession a habit both hazardous and unforgivable: he fell asleep as soon as he was alone. Indeed, he was probably the biggest sleeper in the world. As soon as he was finished eating, he would stretch himself anywhere, on a bench or something, and would not only sleep continuously for three or four hours, but also, as soon as he closed his eyes, he began to snore in a strange way. Nobody could stop laughing, and we often sat there listening to it for hours. It is incomprehensible how many different tones this fellow could produce from his throat and nose without waking

Fig. 7   From *Lotgevallen en vroegere zeereizen* (Amsterdam 1820). The Harbour of St. Denis around 1770 on Réunion Island.

himself up. Sometimes they sounded perfectly like the mooing of an ox, then one thought one heard a fine whistle, and next the deep tone of a French horn, continuing with the rattling of a dying man. In short, he brought forth a quantity of tones that often amused us, but that initially kept everyone who slept near him awake until you got used to it over time. For all that, we almost lost our lives due to the sleeping sickness of this man and might have fallen prey to the waves.

With still weather one can have beautiful nights around the equator, but these can turn into the most violent storms with little warning. There was such delightful weather one night when Sardis had the watch from eight to midnight. The full moon was shining in all its splendor in a bright clear sky. Of the translucence of the skies one can have no idea in Europe. A favorable wind, just enough to fill the sails, which were all open, increased our well-being and let us sigh on with a muffled speed over the rippled surface of the water.

All the passengers and officers amused themselves on deck with singing and their laughter sounded over the wide solitude until, at approximately ten o'clock, one after the other left and went to bed, so Sardis remained on deck alone. He put himself down out of boredom and trusting the good weather he was soon asleep. The sailors of the watch quickly followed their officer's example and crawled into their bunks.

Because of the kindness of the captain I did not sleep with the crew but in one of the fixed births next to the store room that had become available when one of our deck officers died. This favor almost turned out to be fatal and showed me, at least during a terrible half hour, death in its most hideous form.

I had been sleeping for maybe an hour when I was suddenly woken up by something heavy falling on my body. It was the cage of a parrot hanging next to me. I was lying on the bed in a weird posture and thought I heard a frightening and confounded noise around me. Still groggy, I rubbed my eyes to find out whether I was awake or dreaming until I was suddenly wide awake due to the wild cries of our people on the deck, the ringing of the alarm bell, and the roar of the wind. With great difficulty I managed to get out of bed, and then I noticed that the water was one foot high in the cabin. With the ship heeled over thus, I could not stand, and I had to crawl to the door on all fours. All my efforts were in vain because the boxes and suitcases that were pushed against the door from the outside made it impossible to open.

Notwithstanding the confused cries on deck and the howling of the wind, I now heard clearly the call "The axes! Cut the masts! Down with the sails!" It is impossible to give an idea of what was going through me. Great God! What a situation! There I stood, trapped in a berth of five feet wide and seven feet long, forced to await death, which I thought was inevitable because the ship lay almost entirely on one side. The thought of having to die trapped here was even more unbearable than the idea of drowning in the open sea together with my mates. I was desperate.

Suddenly the roar of the wind stopped, but that did not mean the shouting of the officers and the crew abated. On the contrary it grew stronger. A few moments later, I felt the ship start to up-end itself. Finally my frightened shouting was heard by two sailors who were looking for something near me. They managed with some difficulty to remove the chests pushing against my door and released me from my prison.

I found all the passengers standing anxiously huddled together. Once on deck, I saw the sailors busy cutting loose the remainder of the sails and rigging that were still fluttering from the masts. The sea was furious. Yet at that moment a total calm existed. Never did I see a thicker darkness than in this night.

After most of the sails were lowered or, rather, cut off, the vessel straightened itself again. They tried to bring the bow into the wind. Just as this was successful, it seemed as if the storm had been waiting for this sign.

The sound of hundreds of simultaneously fired guns is nothing compared to the ferocious roar of the wind which suddenly put an end to the existing silence. For some moments we couldn't hear or see anything, and we were in a complete state of oblivion. The ship was pushed down by the wind so much that for some time it could not rise above the waves. No human voice, not even using a speaking-trumpet, could be heard at first. The waves rose to unprecedented heights, but our ship, though small, was fortunately well-built and an example of solid workmanship. So we took only a little water on board.

This storm, which continued incessantly for two days, came from the southeast and drove us very far off course. Although we only used a small foresail to keep with the wind, we were very afraid that the storm and the southern currents would run us on to the coast of Madagascar or Africa. We guessed that we were not far off from there.

Finally the wind calmed and the skies cleared. Only then did we learn the true state of affairs which had been the cause of our almost total ruin.

After everyone had left the deck on that beautiful night when the storm broke, two men of the guard who had stayed awake suddenly saw the sky darken with thick clouds. Immediately they went to wake up officer Sardis, but that was easier said than done. He was fast asleep, and the short time it took them was enough to cover the whole sky with the blackest night.

That in a moment of time such a sudden change in the weather can happen is nothing extraordinary in these parts of the world. In these waters one should be very wary. In the best and brightest weather a small cloud sometimes appears on the horizon, at first glance no bigger than a fist. An experienced helmsman has the sails lowered immediately because this cloud, however insignificant it may seem, expands so much in less than fifteen minutes that the sky is completely overcast. It doesn't take long for the fiercest storms to break loose.

Before the required crew had gathered and was ready to stow the sails at Sardis's orders, the wind had suddenly hit the ship with such a terrible force it was tossed directly aside. It was a miracle that nobody went overboard.

Graveyard of the Europeans

Haafner arrived in Batavia on February 4, 1772. He harbored bad memories of the place and wanted to leave as soon as possible. The inconveniences that nature had in store were bearable in Haafner's eyes, but he had little understanding for abuses caused by human failure.

> Now the time drew near when I was to experience all dreadful aspects of disease, dangers, and abuses, and also what man can endure without succumbing to them.
>
> A few days after my arrival I fell ill. The most dangerous symptoms of the dreadful malaria announced themselves. I was delirious for days. My tongue and my whole mouth were covered with a thick black crust. I was very lucky because Captain Bos had me treated by a native doctor, who managed eventually to save me from a certain death.

Now that Haafner had recovered, the captain asked him to return to the Netherlands with his ship. Haafner did not want to go back in his pitiful condition. Rather he wanted to go to India, and he managed to enrol on a ship bound for Bengal. He was assigned light chores in anticipation of the departure of the ship.

> Since I had not yet recovered completely, I mainly had to note down the weighed goods in the warehouses and run errands in the sweltering heat of the city for most of the day. The doctor had expressly forbidden this but I could not avoid it. The result was that after a few days I was overtaken by a new disease. An indescribable inner weakness, a languid slowness together with stiffened and cold limbs made every move I made feel like a rack. To make matters worse I got diarrhea as well.

Soon I was so weak that I could barely stand on my feet. Now I experienced the big difference between my previous captain and this new one. I was completely neglected. They didn't even call a doctor, saying that nature is the best healer. The food I received didn't do anything for my health at all. It consisted of pork, peas, beans, bacon, and other ship's leftovers. Soon I was in a pitiful state, a shadow of my former self. I dragged myself despondently through the house in the oppressive heat and took turns seeking relief in bed and on the street.

Sitting outside he saw the native doctor who had treated him before and called him.

The man had pity on me. He promised to do everything in his power to heal me. He wanted no payment, and that was just as well because I had nothing to give him. The same day he brought me a few medicines. I used these and was cured quickly of the lethargy and weakness which had affected my limbs. The diarrhea had not subsided completely when I was ordered to go on board and we readied ourselves to sail. I would probably have recovered fully if we had stayed in Batavia for another few days because the native doctor was very competent and experienced in his profession. He used only native plants and resources in his practice. European doctors in the Dutch establishments only use medicines from pharmacies back home. They prescribe half-spoiled medicines which have completely lost their effectiveness. Even when they administer the drugs in the correct dose, which due to their profound ignorance rarely happens, they are derived of their healing power and have little or no effect.

A barbers' apprentice who barely knows how to apply a dressing and at most can do a bloodletting, takes a paltry exam which he learns by heart and has himself placed on board a VOC ship as "third master" or "surgeon" as it is called. In case by chance the second surgeon dies during the trip, the ignoramus is appointed in his stead by the captain. I can even give an example in which both the second surgeon and the doctor died during the trip. Because of this, the third master, a funk of 22 years, who just a few months earlier had been soaping the beards of farmers as an apprentice to a village barber, was promoted to doctor. His fortune was made and at the same time the death sentence pronounced on countless victims. Upon arrival in Nagapatnam they made him a doctor of the city hospital, and not long afterwards he became chief doctor of the whole establishment without ever having done any medical study. He was content to learn his job superficially, by practicing cutting the limbs of the victims who ended up under his torturous hands.

It would have been favorable if he had tried by accurately exercising his practice and learning from what occurred in his extensive and deadly practice therewith to compensate his lack of theoretical knowledge. He continued, bloated by prosperity and arrogance, however, to persist in the wrongly learned treatments. Thus he judged with rude insensitivity the most serious cases. He was especially enthusiastic amputating an arm or a leg, charring, and exsanguinations, and actually knew little else. He almost got me in his murderous claws when years later, distraught due to a poisoning, I was looking for anyone of the medical profession to help me. Fortunately, I knew who he was, and as soon as I heard his name and learned what surgery he intended me to undergo without having examined me properly, I immediately sought refuge elsewhere.

This is how the people of the East Indies are treated.

About such abuses little can be found in the archives of the Dutch East India Company because these came under the eyes of the governors of the company. Nor do we find much in the ship logs about blunders committed. It makes reading the deliberately exaggerated stories of Haafner interesting because they not only constitute an additional source of information but at the same time question the reliability of the VOC sources in general (and the studies that quite uncritically elaborate on them in particular). A good example of this is the reason given by Haafner for the sinking of the *Lady Cornelia Jacoba* in the mouth of Hooghly River in Bengal. In the VOC sources it is attributed to errors of the pilot. However, Haafner blames it on the overloading of the ship with private trade goods belonging to the ship's officers which were piled up on the deck. The VOC site, where since 2002 all data on that trading organization has been brought together, mentions Haafner's statement and adds that the official report gave another reading. Haafner had little positive to say on the behavior of the captains on board the ship—in particular, Captain Willem Koelbier, his great tormentor.

Willem Koelbier: The Bloodthirsty Tiger

The character of Captain Koelbier was like that of most captains of the East India Company, who, though not to the extent of that monster, excel in nothing except in cursing, uttering rude expressions and especially abusing the crew. Such a captain has complete power over the ship. He usually rises from sailor or schoolboy to captain. Then one hears him repeating at every opportunity that arises, bloated with pride and arrogance and fully within his rights: "I am master of this ship." On this basis he imposes his will on all. He brooks no contradiction. Everyone blindly obeys his orders. His officers usually imitate the behavior of their master. If he is a torturer then they are too, to please him. However, if he is human, which is a rare phenomenon, they have to control themselves. On the return journey to Europe, at the moment that the Cape has been passed, they temper their bestial behavior, on the one hand to erase the bad treatment from the memory of the crew, and on the other out of fear that the sailors may avenge themselves on arrival in Europe. It happened more than once that a captain was attacked by some sailors in a back alley, sometimes in broad daylight, and thrown into a canal or grievously abused.

With the idea that destiny would be better disposed towards him, Haafner mustered on the *Tempel* which had Nagapatnam (present-day Nagapattinam) on the southern Coromandel Coast, as its final destination. Normally this journey lasted several weeks. This time it would take six months. Haafner only occasionally settles accounts with people, usually without mentioning the full name. Willem Koelbier was an exception because, according to Haafner, he behaved at sea like a beast. It was going to be hell for Haafner who, on the recommendation of an officer whom he was familiar with, was appointed as Koelbier's cabin attendant.

He knew that I had been a cabin attendant on all my travels and that I knew all there is to know about writing and drawing. This was all that was needed to determine Koelbier's choice. He ordered me to follow him into the cabin. In this way things which I had been shielded from now came my way. I fell prey to the daily beatings and cruelties of an insensitive brute.

I was resolved to win his affection through diligence and prompt responsiveness and tried to avert his evil menaces. But in vain. It was not long before I was faced with the reality of his threats.

The second day at my new post he imagined seeing dirt on a couple of plates during lunch. Hereupon he immediately ordered two quartermasters to give me a hundred beatings.

From then onwards rarely a day passed by during which I was not punished, whether by himself or at his command. I tried everything to fulfill my duty to his satisfaction. I wrote his journal, drew portraits and maps of islands and coasts, but it was all in vain. I could not do anything right with that bastard. The most innocent discretion—like not immediately coming to the cabin when he called; breaking a pipe; leaving a drop of water stuck to his glass; or any other such futility—was punished in the cruelest and most disproportionate manner.

Yes, bloodthirsty tiger! I will reveal your main abomination so that anyone who reads this and knows you will be aware with whom they are socializing and see you with the contempt and horror that you deserve. You don't belong in any human society. You should be chained like a wild animal, constantly working and beaten for the rest of your life, punished for your hideous deeds; rather than, in your esteemed public office, infect decent people who do not know you. This unfortunately cannot give back the lives to the many victims of your brutal aggression. The butcher who coolly cuts the throat of the innocent lamb, is in my view much more respectable and more pleasing company than the executioner who derives his existence from torturing and killing people he does not know at all. I despise you.

It was a close call whether would I sooner reach the end of my life then the end of our journey. I almost succumbed to the bloody claws of that despicable Koelbier.

One day I had the bad luck to be alone with him in the cabin, and I did something that he did not like. Without saying a word, while I had my back turned to him, he took a large piece of wood and gave me a terrible blow on my head. Blood gushed from the wound and covered my whole body, and I fainted and fell to the floor.

When I came around, he threw cold water over my face, and I regained my consciousness. It was my good fortune that I was not unconscious for long, because had he feared that he had beaten me to death, he would definitely have thrown me overboard through the cabin window and said that I had fallen out accidentally.

I had a deep wound to the head. It took our ship's doctor a lot of work and three weeks after arriving in Nagapatnam the wound had still not healed. It was the same with my back and thighs which remained marked my entire life from the brutal treatment I underwent aboard the *Tempel*.

After arriving in Nagapatnam Haafner drew up a written complaint that was signed by many crew members and was presented to the governor. To no avail. According to Haafner it was shelved because Koelbier had bribed the governor. In any case, thanks to the fluent pen with which had written the complaint, Haafner could stay in Nagapatnam. He was appointed on September 15, 1773 as the lowest level of clerk, which earned him seven guilders a month. Being freed from the atrocious Koelbier he looked forward to the future again. Koelbier, after returning to the Netherlands, became known as a respectable citizen of Schiedam. Imagine, he devoted himself to the plight of the orphans of the city!

At the Pen in Nagapatnam

Nagapatnam was conquered from the Portuguese in 1658 and the Dutch East India Company had made it headquarters for trading on the Coromandel Coast in the south of India (roughly corresponding with present-day Tamil Nadu). A new fort was built, considered virtually impregnable and manned by a fairly large garrison. The VOC had a string of smaller trading posts along the whole coast such as Porto Novo, Bimilipatnam, Paliacol, Jaggernaikpoeram, and Sadras, where a total of one thousand officials worked. The Coromandel Coast increasingly playing a central role in the trading network of the Dutch East India Company. The production of textiles was concentrated in that area, produced in a wide variety of types and grades.

In the seventeenth century the Dutch started this trade in order to buy spices from the Moluccas. Over time new products such as Japanese copper rods were added. These trade areas were closely connected with each other and were crucial to the VOC, for whom the Coromandel Coast was one of the most important trading territories. In the eighteenth century, especially in the second half, the trade declined. French and British competition undermined the trade of the VOC. The English settled in Madras and Masulipatnam (present-day Machilipatnam) and the French in Pondicherry (now Puducherry). After the Seven Years War (1756–63) the British East India Company began to grow into a regional power that was a direct threat to the VOC.

It did not stop there because turmoil dominated the Indian political scene. The once mighty Mughal Empire, which had reached its greatest expansion in the seventeenth century, went into decline. This allowed regional power centers to emerge. Especially the Muslim Sultanate of Mysore, which after 1761 began an impressive power expansion toward the coast under the leadership of Hyder Ali, threatening the Europeans and forming a counterweight to the English territorial expansionism. After the death of Hyder in 1782, he had a worthy successor in his son Tipu Sultan.

In the 1770s, when Haafner lived and worked in Nagapatnam, these developments were in full swing. The VOC continued to be a formidable power with its Coromandel directorate. At the end of the 1770s a noticeable decline started to set in. The English competition was more palpable every year and the war between Hyder Ali and the British also had an impact on the Dutch establishments. The Fourth Anglo-Dutch War (1780–84), which erupted on the Indian coast in 1781, was the death blow to the Dutch trade. In 1784 Nagapatnam became an English possession and only a few smaller trade establishments on the Coromandel Coast remained in Dutch possession until 1824.

For six years Haafner continued working as a clerk in Nagapatnam. In 1774 his salary was increased to nine guilders per month in view of his "needy state" as it is called in the resolution. He was promoted in 1777, appointed as "absolute assistant" with a salary of 24 guilders per month. In 1779 he was appointed as assistant to the chief administrator Philip Dormieux at a salary of 30 guilders per month. Only towards the end of the 1770s had he somewhat raised himself out of his poor condition, as he called it. In his stories he says little about the period he spent in Nagapatnam, and the VOC archives give only factual information about his career. It is not unlikely that he, like so many VOC officials, traded privately. He mastered bookkeeping which would come in handy later.

For many reasons he later looked back with nostalgia on his life at sea.

> On board I didn't have to bother about my food. I also didn't have to pay rent for a house or room. If I didn't have to keep watch I went to lie down in my bunk and did as I pleased. I had plenty of time to read, write, or practice some science. In the meantime, I kept receiving wages, and I was always owed money. Here, on the other hand I was bound to the lectern from early morning to late evening. Barely finished eating I had to return

> again to the office. Copying and more copying, writing invoices
> and memos, almost always the same. I hated it. On top of this I
> was not used to a sedentary life. I had always been more mobile.

When he was dismissed from the Company's service in September 1779 and
established himself as a free citizen, he could in any case live off his savings for
half a year. His dismissal was connected with cuts with which the Government
in Batavia wanted to reduce costs of the directorate of Coromandel through
the reduction of personnel. As a result, the workforce declined by 40 per
cent. When confronted with the choice to be transferred to Batavia or to
resign from the service, Haafner decided on the latter. The resolution reads
as follows:

> On a request made by the (. . .) absolute assistant Jacob Gotfried
> Hafner is approved and understood to dismiss him from the
> service of the Company with the prolongation of rank and to
> restore him to citizens' freedom with the depreciation of wages
> from today onwards.

On September 15, 1779, Haafner was on his own, a free citizen. He stayed
for several months in Nagapatnam where he learned English from an English
soldier who had deserted. That language increased his opportunity to find
employment with the British. For the time being things would work out
differently.

The Sadras Idyll

On the intercession of the second man in command of Nagapatnam, Johan
Daniel Simons, Haafner managed to get a job in Sadras. That place was 200
kilometers north of Nagapatnam and 60 kilometers south of Madras (present-
day Chennai). Ten VOC employees worked there. Haafner was private
accountant of the administrator of the trade post Jacob Simons, the brother
of Johan Daniel. Sadras was the village that Haafner presents as an example
of the factories along the Indian coasts where people from diverse cultural
backgrounds existed peacefully side by side. Away from the clutches of the
local or colonial authorities, a very lively informal cohabitation had grown up
that can be considered as the best of what the cultural encounter between East
and West has produced. Sadras was the sort of milieu that could develop up in
what I would call the "emporial era", to revive a rather old-fashioned English
word. The emporial era lasted from the beginning of Western explorations in
the new world until the third quarter of the eighteenth century after which

the encounter between East and West turned imperialist. Later Haafner would dream in cloudy Amsterdam of that casual way of life under the palm trees. He invites his readers to take a walk by his hand through his favorite village Sadras. He can't get enough of it.

Accompany me, dear reader! I want to introduce to you Sadras in its earlier prosperity and introduce you to my life, my amusements, and my friends. Offer me the pleasure of telling you about it at length. Alas! I'm so happy to talk about it. The older I get, the happier are the memories of Sadras. Only this remains and gains strength in my memory, while all the other events from my life gradually disappear. It gives me an indescribable pleasure to recall everything down to the smallest detail and to bring to my mind the places, people, their attitudes, and their appearance.

Here was the bleaching field of the Company. Here I often stood to see how young girls, while frolicking and singing, sprayed the outspread linen; how they played, chased each other, and tumbled into the soft sand. How they then jumped into the nearby pond and enjoyed themselves with swimming. The shy nymphs dived under water because I was so nearby. In competition they threw little stones and clay at me which they had picked up from the bottom of the pond with the intent of chasing me away.

There was the indigo factory. The entire perimeter was always covered with a lot of big pots in which the indigo was boiled, transfused, and mixed with lye, lime, sand, and other products to make it suitable for dyeing the linen.

In this street the launderers had their homes. In a lane planted with coconut trees the weavers were living, and all these cabins belonged to the painters of chintzes.

This house under the shade of large overhanging trees was the village school.

How often have I wondered how there were people who wanted to live next to it. You became accustomed to the roar, as you do of other things, otherwise no one would bear it. One cannot imagine what noise the young people make with the recitation of their lessons.

Here a dozen boys rehearse their verses. Next to it again sits a group of boys who loudly intone sentences, and a little further down about thirty of the smallest ones scream their ABCs. Others are doing aloud calculations by heart, and a small club of advanced ones read *puranas* (excerpts from the holy books) in a singsong voice. One examines the other about the lessons, and as an interlude, the quiet-sounding voices of a few young *devadasi*, or temple dancers. Here on the pavement it is teeming with beginners in the art of writing. They sit cross-legged and practice writing letters in the sand while calling them out loud. In a word: everyone screams, all holler, everyone learns by heart as hard as they can. Amidst the deafening din rises occasionally the thundering voice of the master.

Let's remain standing for a while in front of this wide and long street where the bazaar used to be. Previously it was swarming with people. How empty and abandoned it is now!

Never did I make a morning walk without calling at the bazaar. I entertained myself by walking between the double rows of vendors. They ate crouching behind their wares and praised them to the passers-by in a loud or flattering voice.

If it was a big market day, I usually went there very early. I sat on the sidewalk or under a tree and would watch as the inhabitants of Sadras and surrounding villages would flock from all sides laden with their varied merchandise.

Young girls and women with baskets full of fruit and vegetables; men with heavy pots or bags of rice, millet, *nachni* [finger millet] and other grains on their head; old women with crockery, kitchen utensils, mats, and so on; spices, tobacco, betel, and areca merchants; sellers of jiggery sugar (cooked from palm wine, it is black and has an apple flavor), sandalwood, and a lot of other things of which I do not know a tenth.

All rushed to be the first. One ran before the other to get the best place. Finally they sat two rows deep from one end of the market to the other squatting against each other.

Meanwhile, here and there a bit away from the others or on raised platforms, magicians, fortune tellers, tattoo artists, basket makers, and female sellers of coloured glass bangles and very tasty rice flour pancakes seated themselves. The stalls are opened. Traders come up with their touchstone, gold-balance, and bags full of cash, fanams, and rupees and sit down cross-legged under the roof overhang of a house.

The merchants put their linen or other wares on display and the mendicants station themselves as usual at a temple of Ganesh or in front of the house of a Brahmin. A couple of naked fakirs roam around and each tries in his way to attract the attention of the crowd or to appeal to its religious feelings.

It is around nine o'clock. The buyers and the curious arrive. The market becomes turbulent, and there is more rush. It is not long before the whole street echoes with a thousand different cries: Mangos! Ripe mangos! Tamarind! Yellow or ripe bananas! Milk fat! Who wants milk fat! Buffalo milk! Fresh and melted butter! Pickled fruit! Vegetables! Areca and betel! Ripe and fresh coconuts! Fresh palm fruit! Onions! It is an unprecedented jumble of yelling and screaming. The crying of small children; the singing of sannyassins with their rattling cymbals; the drums of the yogis; the shrill bell of the monk singing of the actions of the gods; the oboe of the snake charmers and much more. Then there is the incessant deafening croaking of a thousand crows in this turmoil, grabbing their opportunity, because all are busy haggling, buying, and selling. The sky is black with them and they swarm up and down continuously. If one crow has captured something, he is immediately surrounded by fifty others who want to take it from him. They chase each other, they fight and roll around. They sit in swarms on the low roofs of the houses and the trees. With elongated necks and wings half spread they lean forward and lie in wait for a chance to steal a banana or other fruit, or a cake or something. A little further on is a gang that attacks the exhibited cereals while their companions buzz around the head of the merchant, hitting him in his face with their wings while flying by to confuse him. There they have a woman or girl who has something or other to their taste completely surrounded. Above her, behind her and alongside her they are hopping back and forth and she must constantly beat with a branch to keep them away. One cannot imagine how bold and cunning this brood is.

The proud temple bull makes his way through the crowd. Here he picks up a mouth full from one vegetable seller, there from another. They leave him be. They even offer him the best and finest. They try to lure him because everyone feels honored by his visit.

Advanced Science

Haafner felt completely at home in Sadras. It offered more attractions than Nagapatnam. He often spoke with a sanyassin from whom he learned the basic principles of Sanskrit and who convinced him to become a vegetarian. The sanyassin lived near Sadras in the ruins of Mahabalipuram, a huge city which dated from the time of a long lost civilization. When Haafner lived in Sadras, he had often visited these nearby ruins. According to the Dutch Indologist Jean Philippe Vogel, Haafner's descriptions of the temple complexes were the first and most accurate of his time. The thought of the place brought Haafner in a melancholic romantic mood:

> We saw the mountains of Mahabalipuram ahead of us and around two o'clock in the afternoon we entered the valley and found ourselves almost at the center of this large collection of marvels.
>
> What an amazing scenery for anyone who comes here for the first time! His contempt for the people of India can be ever so great and he can be heavily biased against them, but as soon as he has seen Mahabalipuram, he will have to admit that these people must have had a high level of civilization. That the arts and sciences have previously experienced a flourishing and that everything we call miraculous like the pyramids of Egypt cannot be compared with the awe-inspiring ruins and colossi that can be found in Mahabalipuram and spread across all of India.
>
> In this valley it is always teeming with all kinds of birds in more numbers than I've ever seen anywhere else. From hill to hill echoes the cooing of the innumerable turtledoves that nest in the cracks of the rocks and the hollows of the ruins without being disturbed.

Haafner climbed one of the hills and from the pinnacle he enjoys the scene that unfolds before him:

> My imagination carried me back to the days of antiquity, to unknown and bygone ages when the great Yudhishthira ruled here, and from here sent out his commands to all corners of his vast empire.
>
> These awesome ruins, these grandest monuments from time immemorial filled my soul with sadness.
>
> What an irrefutable proof of the futility and inconstancy of sublunary things is reflected in the once great and mighty, now derelict buildings. Compare their former glory and present ruin!

Where is the city of the twenty gates and one hundred palaces? What is left of its former glory and splendor and what remained of its many inhabitants?

The beautiful and magnificent city of the invincible Yudhishthira has decayed to a miserable little village. In small straw huts a few poor Brahmins now live there. This area is now dominated by a foreign power and the unfortunates who dwell in it today groan under the slavish tyranny of the Europeans.

Nothing of this famous city is left but the awesome buildings that form the sad skeleton of the former grandeur.

Loneliness and deathly silence now take the place of the incessant noise of innumerable crowds that used to swarm here together. The songs, the celebrations, the processions, and the sacrifices to the gods have fallen silent. The temples stand forlorn, overgrown by dense impenetrable scrubbery. Snakes and lizards live there, and the fierce viper nests here. From the walls hang withered vines and braids of ivy. Brown moss covers the walls, but through the hollow temples the wind now whistles, and where the songs and cheers echoed, one now hears the night owl.

It may be here on this road that the victor Yudhishthira sat on his chariot drawn by elephants, surrounded by his warriors, returned triumphant over his enemies, or the other way, went to war to punish them. Here he showed himself to his subjects to do justice and to hear their complaints. Here possibly stood the heralds proclaiming his praise and inviting the people to public celebrations. But all the pomp and circumstance of the court, all the palaces and triumphal arches are gone! Even the name of the great prince and his successors can only be found in the mysterious fabulous stories of the *Mahabharata*.

Is this the destiny of human effort? Must his work created by thousands of hands with unspeakable effort and patience thus perish into nothingness? Must his actions, his glory be submerged in oblivion?

O Mahabalipuram! It is in your school that the vain and imperious learn to be humble. They can learn more here than all of what is being said by philosophers and theologians on the vanity and inconstancy of terrestrial things. In this mood, with my heart full of thoughts of impermanence, I left the hill and returned to the valley.

Fig. 8   From *Reize in eenen Palanquin*, vol. 1 (Amsterdam 1808). The ruins of
Mahabalipuram.

That Haafner was subject to mood swings is evident from the following short
excerpt in which he ascribes more continuity to the work of man after he had
done more research.

> These old buildings clearly show the then advanced degree of
> science and civilization of the Indians. One cannot help but
> think reverently about the greatness and power of nations which
> have been able to build and complete such giant structures.
>
> All-destructive time, and the even more destructive hand
> of man, has caused little damage up to now. This is certainly
> due to the manner of the buildings' construction. For centuries
> they have been there and they will be for many more. The
> underground rooms and caves will probably disappear only with
> the destruction of the world, or of the mountains in which they
> have been dug or chiseled.
>
> It was already getting dark when we returned from our
> walk—or rather call it a clambering party over rocks and hills.
> We had barely seen a twentieth part of the ruins. In order to
> accurately investigate all, one needs at least a week or longer.

Sadras Lost, Disastrous Cost

The British raid on Sadras at the outbreak of the Fourth Anglo-Dutch War came like a bolt from the blue. While the party in honor of the birthday of Jakob Pieter de Neijs, the Dutch resident, was in full swing, on June 29, 1781, tragedy hit. In one stroke the feasting and partying became something of the past. The next day the Dutch found themselves being transported to Madras as prisoners of war, and they had to watch with sorrow how Sadras became victim of the scorched earth tactics of the British.

How different it was when Haafner lived there.

> O! most entertaining time of my life! Care and sorrow free days that will never return again. Why were you of such short duration? All pleasurable expectations and joyful outlook with which I delighted my soul were never fulfilled.
>
> I had hoped that Sadras would mean the end of my misfortunes and nomadic existence. I thought to find a safe haven for the setbacks that fate always had in store for me and to see all my wishes fulfilled. Empty imagery! Chimeras of happiness! How everything changed and turned into the opposite.

Haafner takes us back to the informal and social life he had experienced while living in Sadras.

> For example, in the evening there is a party at Thomasio Cruz's celebrating his wife's birthday. We were all invited and the whole group goes to his house. It is already crowded and everyone welcomes us. Cigars are lighted. The formal coats are removed and people make themselves comfortable. Beer, punch, arak, lemonade stand in a separate room on a large table. They drink as much and whatever they want. You look among the ladies for your beloved, your girlfriend, an acquaintance, or something more than that. You give her all attention, serve her, and try to entertain her by saying all kinds of nice things. The one tries to outdo the other in witticisms, funny stories, and jokes. Laughter is all around. It is life and joy that reigns and everyone indulges in it without any restraint.

Haafner would return a few years after Sadras' destruction. There was virtually nothing left of Sadras, and melancholically he makes a walk through the past and remembers not only the feasts that were given. He sketches a lively picture of a village scene. Together with the following quote, it forms a unique snapshot of a bygone society, totally unique in eighteenth-century travel literature.

Their dilapidated houses in which I had been so well entertained and received with much joviality, our comfortable society is called back once again to my memory. How quickly everything can change! I could not call it back to mind, it seemed like a dream.

Here lived hospitable Barlou with his handsome and kind wife. In this room we often sat around the floral mat in the middle of which a piled-up rice dish steamed, the pleasant aroma of the spices rising up from the tasty curry. How jovially he invited us to dine. And then his amiable Suzon! How diligently she served everyone. The one she gave atchar of mashed shrimp from Malacca, or atchar of mango from Bimilipatnam, and the other she gave homemade sambal, or sambal with spicy pepper water. A deep silence fell on the eager eaters until full glasses went round and the hot punch loosened their tongues. It was followed by a bout of toasting. The glasses were raised and loud hoorays reverberated through the entire village!

This was the home of the happy De Lange where continuous joy reigned, where there was no place for mourning and agonizing worry. From nightfall until late at night the fiddle was played, and from afar one could hear the clattering cymbals. De Lange was also an accomplished guitar player who could extract sweet tones from it. Weekly lithe dancers gathered with him, and agile youth practiced there. How the young girls pattered with impatience as the rustling music sounded the contra dance! How kind and excited they were when one accompanied them on the dance floor while their parents rejoiced over the agility of their children. They nodded to each other and fondly reminisced the time when they were young.

And you amusing Seidler! You excelled in entertaining tales and witty remarks. With your funny behavior you often had a boisterous party erupt in laughter and brought the whole table in an uproar. Seidler was an inexhaustible source of amusing histories and witty tales. Sometimes the intently listening guests forgot to eat, or misplaced the food they were bringing to their mouth. Now your home is completely dilapidated. Even you are not here anymore! In the prime of your life you had to descend into the grave.

On the corner of this street the house of the one-eyed commander of our garrison is still standing. He was at the same time also landlord and innkeeper. He was always cheerful and jovial despite his wicked wife who made his life miserable. She was on top of that also ugly, terribly jealous, and drank her shot of arak with the best.

Haafner compares the informal Sadras society with the formal European one:

Disappear you stiffly organized gatherings with your card tables, your empty flattering, your ceremonies, your muddled thoughts where everything is going by rank and position. Where one only comes together to smoke tobacco and drink wine, all by the measure and at its time. Everyone is happy when those annoying boring meetings are over and they can return home.

In Sadras ease, jocularity and gaiety prevailed. No exaggerated formality. No ceremony, no rank, no titles. Only friendship brought us together and the one sought to entertain the other. Everyone strove to improve the atmosphere as much as possible. I have never regretted being in the company of *mestizos*. I was never bored and the night was over before I realized it.

The picture of destruction Haafner paints is fully confirmed in a report from 1786 by Willem Blauwkamer, the Governor of the Coromandel coast, to the Heeren XVII (the Council of 17) of the VOC.

Sadras makes a sad spectacle. The English demolished the fortress after they had taken it and then abandoned it. Afterwards it fell prey to the marauding bands of Hyder Ali Khan who finished the work of the English by ruining everything and by murdering or deporting the remaining inhabitants. Many died of hunger and misery if they didn't have the luck to find shelter elsewhere. This fine establishment has become a wilderness and a shelter for ravenous beasts.

Sadras never recovered from the blow and is now a small fishing village. The Dutch fort and its two small warehouses have been restored, as a potential tourist attraction. Two nuclear power plants nearby might stand in the way of Sadras becoming a touristic hot spot.

Chapter 3

Where can Our Soul Shelter?

In early July 1781, Haafner arrived with other Dutch prisoners of war in Madras. That city was completely inundated by refugees as a result of the war between the British and Hyder Ali Khan. That war had brought all economic activity to a complete standstill. Because there was no harvesting, food had become astronomically expensive. What little rice was available in the city came from Bengal by sea. A commission established by the British governor George Macartney to take stock of the food situation, concluded on July 7 that, according to the official information, there was food for just two days. Black marketeering was rife. This situation continued till the middle of 1783 and is known in the annals of the history of Madras as the Great Famine.

It is therefore not surprising that Haafner, who had been robbed of all his property, tried to recover 1,000 pagodas that he had lent to Jakob Pieter De Neijs, the Dutch commander of Sadras. Haafner was beside himself with rage when De Neijs refused to pay back the advance and wrote an angry letter to him: "It is impertinent to behave in such a way with someone to whom your honor has so many obligations." Haafner's distress increased even further when his friend Ernst Wieder died, and he felt a moral obligation to take care of the widow Wieder and her children. That was not without self-interest, because he was in love with her *mestizo* daughter, Anna, with whom he was indeed later involved. From the letter it can also be gathered that Haafner had not only started working as a bookkeeper for Stephan Popham, barrister and attorney of the Madras government, but also for the exceedingly rich Portuguese merchant Antonio de Souza. They were among the most influential individuals in Madras. Skilful accountants were rare on the Coromandel Coast, so Haafner quickly found employ.

Haafner had access to the highest circles of Madras through Popham and he would let this be known to his former superiors. He did not fail to use his contacts to pressurize De Neijs and demanded he sign a statement in which the legitimacy of his financial claim was confirmed. He also wrote a letter to George Mackay, the mayor of Madras, in which he demanded the money that De Neijs owed him from the British Government. Mackay replied that he had forwarded the claim to the appropriate authorities. He also made it clear he was not pleased with the tone of Haafner's letter. "The insolence and impertinence of your letter ill becomes you, and be assured will do you no good."

Famine in Madras

From late December 1781 the living conditions in Madras further deteriorated. The city was surrounded by soldiers of Hyder Ali Khan and the supply of food had come entirely to a halt because of the inaccessibility of the city by sea from October to January due to the monsoon. On February 14, 1782 a French fleet under Admiral Pierre André de Suffren appeared totally unexpectedly along the coast of Madras. He surprised the British fleet under Admiral Edward Hughes. The battle of February 17, which happened within sight of Madras, remained inconclusive. The initiative, which until then had been with the English, passed to the French. De Suffren subsequently succeeded to take Trincomalee on the east coast of Ceylon on August 30, 1782, which had been captured by the British from the Dutch in 1781.

With the arrival of a second French fleet, which had a large military contingent on board led by old India hand General Charles Joseph Patissier de Bussy, the fate of the British Empire in India seemed sealed. De Suffren wrote: "*Je me crus maître de l'Inde*," that he believed himself to be the master of India. The British writer William Hickey, who was captured by the French in Ceylon, also thought it looked bleak for the empire:

> This was a melancholy history for me, and from the fall
> of Trincomalee, as well as Suffren's fleet appearing to ride
> triumphant and unopposed in those seas, I really feared it was
> but too true, and that the British sun was near setting in the East.

That fear had also overcome the English in Madras. At the end of September 1782 the city government was forced to begin the deportation of 200,000 refugees who had sought refuge and were living in and around the city. Hickey, who had been released and had arrived in Madras, gives an eyewitness report:

> A true melancholy spectacle met our sight, at which my dearest
> Charlotte [his wife] was affected beyond measure, the whole
> road being strewed on both sides with the skulls and bones of

the innumerable poor creatures who had there laid themselves down and miserable perished from want of food.

Haafner, who had been told in June by the British Government that his financial demands would not be honored, wanted to get away from the city given the desperate situation. De Neijs, who was to leave for Batavia with the ship *Concordia* together with a large number of Dutch prisoners of war, could not resist spiting Haafner:

> I regret your honor so badly succeeded with the English government, and it surprises me that Mr. De Souza who after all has so much influence was not able to achieve anything in your advantage.

Haafner saw little use in traveling to Batavia and decided to wait for another opportunity.

The arrival of a large fleet with provisions from Bengal around October 10 raised the expectation of an improvement of the food situation in the city.

> The joy these glad tidings caused among the desperate and suffering crowd cannot be described in words. Loud shouts of joy resounded in all the streets. A multitude of people thronged the shore and raised their hands to heaven in gratitude. Women and children, everyone insisted on seeing the ships. The one pointed them out to the other. The cheering was ubiquitous.

Those hopes were dashed by a terrible cyclone that hit Madras on October 14 and 15, 1782. The entire fleet of 105 ships was lost and with it the rice. Haafner blames the English for this disaster because they, despite the obvious signs of an impending storm, refused to give permission to unload the ships. The *Indian Gazette*, one of the first newspapers published in Asia, reported on November 9, 1782:

> It is impossible to describe a scene of such horror and distress! The howling of the wind, the roaring of the surf, with the cries of drowning people, and the beach for some miles strewed with wrecks and dead bodies.

Haafner saw it with his own eyes and becomes furious at the thought of the behavior of the English.

> Who can describe the despair that engulfed the "doomed" people when all the food had washed away, when the ships had sunk and the hope of life had been completely shattered?

It's hard to believe that just at that moment the English suddenly stopped selling food which hitherto they had auctioned with a cruel pity. They closed the warehouses on the grounds that they did it out of concern for the English and the garrison.

Now nowhere, except from hellish usurers who conspired with members of the British government, could the people still buy a little food at extremely outrageous prices.

The poor refugee or resident of Madras often gave away his entire fortune to those monsters to, if even for once, satisfy the hunger of his family.

From then on their misery increased at every sunrise, and their suffering rose from hour to hour.

Exposed to pouring monsoon rains, the helpless families sat huddled together under whatever passed for shelter. Trembling, powerless, and without food crowded together they sat there as heartbreaking wails rose to the sky. Repeatedly people lost consciousness until finally the convulsive death smothered their anxious voice, squeezing their sighing heart as one fell over another.

The streets were littered with dead and dying. Of such horrors, one can have no idea. I can never forget, they are still hounding my mind to this very day.

The situation in Madras worsened day by day. The governor Macartney noted on October 31 that every day hundreds of people were dying and that the situation was extremely critical. According to Haafner the situation became intolerable. He paints the situation with a Goya-like poignancy.

I felt I was succumbing and hastened to get through. Suddenly I saw a woman as thin as a skeleton sit behind a collapsed wall. Beside her lay the body of a man, and in her hands—it still haunts me when I recall it—she held a dead infant. I watched as with her bloody teeth she took a bite out of its body. As a starving tigress she tore off the little flesh that covered the tender members of the baby. A cold shiver ran through my veins! My hair stood on end! I felt my knees sink from under me.

The only safe haven in the proximity that was still free from the war was Ceylon. Haafner knew friends who had fled there, so he decided to do the same. It took him much effort, and he succeeded in embarking in a boat; but cannon shots across the bow forced him to return to the harbor. Once ashore, he was immediately arrested and was taken for a French spy. He caused a riot.

> It was almost ten o'clock when we arrived at the office of the provisions master on the beach. It was full of people: half the city knew that a spy had been captured. Everyone wanted to see him. "Here he is! Here he is!" I heard from all sides. In an instant I was surrounded by people, all thronged around me. "Who are you?" ten voices asked at the same time. "Who is he?" others cried. "Yes it is a spy," said one, and "It's a Dutchman, I know him," said the other. "It is an honest man, I'll answer for it," I heard a familiar voice say. It was my friend Frank.

Meanwhile the provisions master Hall entered, who struck a very different tone than Frank. He began to interrogate Haafner:

"Who are you?" He asked in a gruff voice, as soon as he saw me.

I: A Dutchman from Sadras.

He: Where is the permit?

I: I did not know I needed one. I do not have any.

He: What, no permit! you probably do not know that I'm provisions master and no one is allowed to leave the harbor without my knowledge?

I: My Lord! I humbly beg you to take into consideration that I am a stranger....

He: What stranger! Excuses, nothing but excuses. You should know the laws of the country where you are. You do not steel away from the harbor like a thief without any evil intention. You are possibly the spy of the French dogs? We'll get it out of you.

I: My Lord! I said, looking at him firmly, I was never a spy and never will be a spy. I will show you a hundred people who will testify that I am an honest man.

Fortunately for Haafner, his friend Frank was able to convince the provisions master that he had no evil intent. He was taken to the governor for further questioning. This one let him go as long as he would accept the mission of handing some letters over personally to a certain Colonel Alexander Hamilton in Tranquebar, a Danish settlement further down the coast. For this he would receive 1,000 pagodas.

> I showed myself very willingly and accepted the assignment, as
> one may well imagine, with apparent pleasure.

Haafner knew in advance that he would not carry the mission out, however
much he needed the 1,000 pagodas. He was given permission to leave. The
journey led him down the coast via Covelam, Sadras, and Alampara where,
having come ashore, he was taken prisoner by a cavalry regiment of Hyder Ali
Khan. Fortunately for Haafner, he could prove that he had saved the leader
Rosan Ali Kahn from the hands of the English during the time he stayed in
Sadras. He was released. After arriving in Pondicherry he handed over the
letters to Étienne André de Solminihac, the provisions master of Pondicherry,
whom Haafner describes as follows:

> I entered into a side room. I saw a small portly man, as round
> as a barrel, sitting at a writing desk. His head was covered with
> a white cotton cap that hung over one ear. He was naked except
> for a shirt and underpants and wore slippers without socks.
>
>   His strange appearance confused me a bit. He seemed to
> notice this. "Yes, yes, it is me," he exclaimed. "You are not the
> first one to be astonished at my négligée but because of the heat
> I always walk around like this in the house. How unhappy you
> are when you're so fat. *Mais, l'habit ne fait pas le moine.*

The Foolish Count Bonvoux

Haafner immediately continued his journey, and having arrived in Tranquebar
he found the family Wieder who had fled earlier. The mother entrusts her
daughter to Haafner, who couldn't be happier. With his beloved Anna he
makes the crossing to the relative safety of Ceylon. On this journey they were
accompanied by a rather headstrong French count, and this was almost fatal.
In telling this story years later, Haafner is at his best. By now he knows how
to administer and build narrative tension skillfully, and the count emerges as
a real vibrant literary character. The following fragments don't do full justice
to the dramatic structure of the story, which follows a pattern often used by
Haafner, alternating misery and enthusiasm. They do provide a picture of
how the twelve-man crew was tossed between hope and despair on a journey
that took a week when it should have taken a day.

   Haafner first pokes fun at the count who asked him if he could travel with
him.

I could not stop myself from laughing heartily at his servants. A count and Knight of Malta, because he was that as well, who was traveling together with a kitchen maid and a laundress. To Anna and her mother, who were present at the conversation between me and the count, I concisely explained it in the Malabar language. It made them laugh heartily. He didn't mind. "It is my habit," he said. "I always travel with a laundress and a kitchen maid. The one serves me, the other prepares my food. It is natural to me. *D'Ailleurs*," he continued looking at me meaningfully, "*le nom ne fait rien à la chose, vous le verrez*".

Initially Haafner did not like the idea but he let himself be persuaded by the sweet talk of the count. It was the beginning of all misery, because Haafner discovered after one day at sea that the count had only brought provisions for one day. Haafner discovered this after they had enjoyed a rich dinner abundantly accompanied with wine. At that moment there was still full hope that they would reach Jaffnapatnam (now Jaffna) by the next day, but when Haafner woke up the next day, the land had disappeared from sight. According to the skipper, it was because the count had forced him to change course. Jacob tried to seek redress from the verbose and careless count, who shrugged off Haafner's comments.

Several times I wanted to cut him off but he wouldn't let me speak. I could have hit him on the head! "Come out from under the tent," I finally cried impatiently, "and see for yourself! I don't want to hear your nonsense talk any longer." After this I went back on deck.

Shortly thereafter he followed me with his map in one and his binoculars in the other hand. After having searched the entire horizon and seeing nothing else than sea and sky, he was lost for words.

"Well count, now what!" I asked him, "What do you think? Shall we still in a few hours have breakfast in Ceylon?"

He shrugged and referred to his map. "However, the course is south-east, as one ...." "Count!" I bitterly cut him short. "Not I, but you, have less knowledge of the compass and naval affairs than your maid. Anyway, what business do you have with the rudder and the course? You're just a passenger and you have nothing to command. That is up to me and the skipper. And if you wanted to be involved in it, you should know that coastal vessels like ours must keep to the coast as much as possible not to be swept away by the strong currents coming from the Gulf of Manaar."

"What currents?" he replied, "There are no currents because then they should have been drawn on the map with an arrow. See here...."

"Go to hell with your arrow and map!" I cried angrily. "I wish you had never set a foot on this vessel. Your avarice and foolishness have exposed us to hunger and the greatest threat to our lives. If we float past the northeast corner of Ceylon, we are lost."

Haafner then ordered the crew to row back towards land, but that attempt led to nothing, and the atmosphere was depressed.

We sat looking at each other with sorrowful and sad faces. Anna was worried, the count grumpy and angry, and I was all of that together. No one spoke, and if anything was said, it was usually a wish for wind.

But there was no wind. Towards the evening a little wind arose. Just enough to ensure we stayed in the same place, and the rowers could rest their weary limbs. They had rowed all day in the blazing sun and eaten nothing more than raw rice mixed with water.

I feared that Anna would not be able to eat this but she managed. To eat raw rice with water or wine, good teeth are necessary, and great hunger is required. That we didn't lack, and probably no one on board couldn't except for the count, who was badly endowed as far as teeth were concerned. He did not have any molars in his mouth and the remaining four or five teeth were not very good either.

It took four days before Haafner could finally cry "land in sight". In the meantime, he had many altercations with the count, who even attacked him with a sword and thereby fell overboard. The crew didn't want to save him, but Haafner could not find it in his heart to let the count drown. He received no gratitude for that, because they had hardly reached the mainland of Ceylon when the count attacked him.

His shot had only just missed me, and I flew towards him like an arrow from the bow. He threw the empty gun to my head, but I dodged it. Now he waved with his cane to keep me at a distance. I ignored it, because he could hit me only once. Even for that I did not leave him the time. I threw my hat in his face and struck him. There lay the count stretched out on the sand.

After this the count disappears from sight, and Haafner continues his journey over water to Jaffnapatnam. At last he could enjoy being together with Anna in peace.

Anna's Embrace

Now we proceeded back aboard our boat. Just the two of us alone under the tent. Nobody was bothering us; no count, no laundress or kitchen maid, no troublesome witnesses who dared spy or peep! The monotonous chant of the rowers, the thud of the oars, the soft rustle and murmur of water around our boat, the melodious cries of woodcocks, the voices of people that occasionally rose from the banks. Everything instilled a gentle sensation, a sweet and soothing passion.

Oh unforgettable night! River of Kayts never can I mention your name without remembering I tasted happiness on your waters! Moments of pleasure! Your effect on the heart of the people is enduring and how quickly you may be over, your impression continues even longer in the memory than those of sadness and grief.

I forgot all my decisions, all my intentions, all my fears and anxious prospects; homeland, friends, everything I forgot in Anna's arms.

Thus Haafner arrived on an island that had been firmly in Dutch hands for over a hundred years. The battle with the Portuguese for Ceylon which had erupted in 1640 with the battle of Galle had come to an end in 1658 with the conquest of Jaffnapatnam by the VOC. The VOC had conspired with the king of Kandy who ruled the interior. The VOC controlled the coastal strip with an extensive system of defenses whose remnants are still visible today. Galle Fort with its 12 bastions has been preserved almost completely and is on the UNESCO Cultural Heritage list. The VOC exported mainly cinnamon, shark skins, elephants, and pearls. After Java, Ceylon, with its capital Colombo, was the main settlement of the VOC in Asia and played a major role in the inter-Asian trade.

But starting in 1750 the power of the Dutch East India Company began to wane. The King of Kandy saw his chance and with the support of the

British attacked the VOC. This turned into a veritable colonial war that lasted from 1760 to 1765 and cost the VOC 2 million guilders. The peace preserved the status quo of Dutch rule, which prevailed at the time of Haafner's arrival. The severe blow of the Fourth English War marked the beginning of the end of the VOC rule in Ceylon. In 1796 England conquered the island, and at the Peace of Amiens in 1802 Ceylon was ceded to England. Haafner later wrote, against the background of the negotiations leading to the Peace of Amiens in 1801, an article in the *Vaderlandsche Letteroefeningen* entitled "Something about the Island of Ceylon" in which he argued for the retention of the beautiful island.

Fig. 9   Title page of *Lotgevallen op eene reize van Madras over Tranquebar naar het Eiland Ceilon* (Haarlem 1806). Jacob Haafner and Anna Wieder together with crew arriving on Ceylon in 1782.

After the rigors of the sailing trip, Haafner found himself suddenly in an earthly paradise that lay within a stone's throw from the battlefield. Jaffnapatnam, located in an amphitheater on the Palk Strait, was, according to contemporary descriptions, one of the most attractive places on earth. That had not always been so, because the Dutch had furiously battled the Vanni, the local population. The area was pacified in the beginning of the eighteenth century only after the so-called Vanni fort system was completed. What the Vanni were then the Tamil Tigers were a decade ago: Jaffnapatnam and the area around it was turned into a battleground and was largely destroyed as a result of the bombing of the Sri Lankan army.

Around 1780 many old friends of Haafner had sought refuge there from war, like the master cooper Templijn, a friend from Nagapatnam. He had bought a coconut palm grove which was situated on a wide tree-lined avenue on the edge of the town. Haafner was able to buy a similar garden next to it, and he built a house for Anna and himself.

> Here I lived without fear and content, free from all care, sorrow and grief. In my life, there were few moments when I felt as happy as in Jaffnapatnam. No wonder. I had everything that can make a man happy in this world. I had money enough to live for a very long time, and in father Templijn I had a sincere man as a friend.
>
> I have always considered independence the greatest and most precious gift. It had become mine. No one had anything to say over me. I did not have to fear, flatter or envy anybody. I was completely my own lord and master. I loved the outdoors, and my wish was also in that respect fulfilled. The garden or villa that I lived in had at the rear an orchard packed with high rustling palm and coconut trees, and in the front a vegetable and flower garden. A simple cottage stood in the middle of the garden. I had always wanted to have a sweet girlfriend who passionately loved me without ulterior motives and to whom I could give myself without the least restraint. I had her in my Anna. She animated everything that surrounded me. In her enchanting company my days flowed by, soft and gentle like a clear stream between flowery banks.
>
> Enchanted images of that time, appear again! Come and surround me again with your captivating shadows. Pleasant hours and comfortable days of Jaffnapatnam! Ah, rise again from the sea of oblivion and come back to my mind in all your bright colours!

Every morning and evening Haafner made a stroll along the Palk Strait which separates the Jaffna peninsula from Ceylon. At four he gets up and starts on his way.

> How pleasant, how delightful is the lovely morning. What a powerful and irresistible influence it has on the nature of all

creatures. How joyful and happy is all nature! Everything awakens as with a new life. Millions of living creatures emerge from their hiding places. How the early crows dive by the hundreds from all sides with confused cries out of trees and swarm together in wide and bewildered circles. The buzz of their feathers is like that of the blades of a windmill. See how the mountain eagle widely spreads its wings. He leaves his perching place and rises with slow strokes to greet the rising sun.

Here I stand on the bank of the Palk Strait and look, just like the rest of all creation around me, eagerly awaiting the appearance of the queen of the day. See! How graceful and benevolent she rises from behind the flat expanse of water. In quiet radiance she rises and envelops everything in light! How delightful she shines on the forests, spreads her rays over the plains and gilds the tops of the tall palm, coconut, and areca trees! Slowly and majestically she enters in full splendor upon her blue path. Light clouds with gilded edges surround her. Every moment her glow increases and the dew-covered plants are already feeling the impact of her rays nurturing them.

How delighted and with how much pleasure I walked along this beautiful cove. How the small rushing waves shine in the morning sun! How beautiful is the varied green of the many tree species which are mirrored in the water along the shore. The pure blue sky, the dense thickets, here and there groups of high leafy trees, the gentle murmur of water; everything fills the soul with unspeakable tender sensations and sweet perceptions.

But toward the evening, when the sun has nearly completed its course and the cooling sea breeze tempers the heat of the day, this place acquired a new kind of fascination for me. In the company of Anna I often visited these entertaining shores. While frolicking and playing she hunted the little crabs on the sandy shore and sought sponges, horns, and turtles with which the banks are covered, I sat myself down under a tall palm or coconut tree.

The Palmetto

The book that Haafner published on his time in Ceylon, *Journey on Foot through the Island of Ceylon* began with a 60-page description of land, people, history, flora, and fauna of Ceylon. This was more a romantically colored account than that it was an attempt to come to the knowledge of the world in the manner of the Encyclopedists. But it is not without interest. Haafner does for example give a plausible explanation for the death of baron Lubbert Jan van Eck, who was governor of Ceylon and who plunged the VOC into a five-year colonial war (1760–65). The official sources attributed his death to a heart attack, but Haafner says he committed suicide, a plausible explanation in the light of the complete failure of van Eck's expedition to Kandy. Haafner also devotes several pages to the original population of the Ceylon, the Vanni. Yet he is strongest in his lyrical description of the palm tree which he cherished as a symbol of life in the tropics and a universe in itself:

> And you who are [the coconut tree's] equal in beauty and even surpass him in utility. Lush palm! Just as the coconut tree you grow in infertile soil and allow other fruit trees to grow in your shadow, and you too wear your beautiful crown at your elevated crest. No low-growing branches disfigure your slender stem and your long, curved, fan-shaped leaves serve as roofs for houses or fencing for the garden of your owner. When the leaves are cut into long strips, you can write a message on them to distant friends and acquaintances with an iron stylus (…) also [the palm tree] gives the sweet blue wine which when drunk in moderation is very healthy and has cured many horrible diseases.
>
> It is pleasant to visit the dense palm forest with the dawning of the day, as the flaming world-torch rises from the eastern horizon, and its long slanting rays spread a purple glow over trees and fields, or when she hurries to the west and has lost most of her power. How often, when the oppressive heat of the afternoon was reduced and the cool evening breeze rustled through the trees, I strolled to the alluring palm forest in the company of young friends. Then we looked until we saw the leaning ladder of a clambering palm-wine tapper. Frisky and merry we sat down under the gentle tree and with joyful cheering proclaimed our arrival to the lofty cup bearer. With loud cries he replied to us from the arched top and soon slipped down with the filled gourd. Then we handed round the foaming pot and drank while smoking cigars and making jokes, often sounding laughter through the woods until we were satisfied with the harmless blue wine. Thus we spent our time until dusk started and the winged citizens of the air went to sleep in their nests.

Then we returned by the narrow paths through the undulating paddy fields.

Oh, That Wanderlust!

There seemed little reason for Haafner to leave this place. And yet despite the fortunate circumstances in which he found himself, Jacob became restless.

> Yes, how foolish and insane it will seem to the reader, the wish to venture in search of the ferocious and wild animals of Ceylon and to get to know them, especially the elephants, in their natural state, had often overwhelmed me since my arrival in Jaffnapatnam […] But there was little opportunity that my wish and desire would be fulfilled. To roam around the immense forests on my own would have been extremely foolish. I would have been lost the first day and would have starved or would have been torn to bits by the monsters that live there. It was certain that no European would be foolish enough to accompany me on such a journey without a goal, without a plan, without the prospect of financial gain. That's why I kept my mouth shut because such a journey seemed as impossible to me as a trip to the moon.

When his friend Templijn asked Haafner to go with him to Colombo where Templijn wanted to work as a master cooper, Haafner did not hesitate a moment. Now he could surrender to that nature which he described as travel fever.

> O! that wanderlust is an unfortunate incurable disease that does not end other than with life itself, which often is shortened by it, or when due to old age, defects, or domestic circumstances no longer is able to answer its call. I have been afflicted by that disease from my youth. She haunts me even now that I am old and she blights many a day. This insatiable curiosity to want to investigate everything myself and this romantic mad passion for strange encounters and adventures. Into how much danger they have plunged me and how much sorrow and adversity they have caused me. How often have I been thrown into misfortune by it or removed from the happiness I already enjoyed.

Immediately they began to prepare for the journey along the west coast of Sri Lanka. Haafner went to the commander of Jaffnapatnam, Barholomeus

Jacobus Raket, of whom he got a so-called *oppa*. That is a palm leaf document in which the chiefs of the villages were commanded in Tamil and Sinhalese to provide the holder of the *oppa* with food and a place to sleep for a fee. In comparison with the rest of the preparations, this was a trifle. Provisions for three weeks had to be arranged and a lot of other things. They agreed to meet on the morning of departure in the garden of Templijn.

> Our first concern was the distribution of luggage and food between the carriers and to assign to each his burden. For the transport of the important victual, rice, we chose the three strongest coolies. Each of them was laden with 60 pounds, which they carried from a bamboo pole slung over their shoulders. Two others took the suitcase of d'Allemand and the sixth had two large copper pots with narrow necks each containing about a bucket of water. The seventh coolie carried two baskets in which our liquor, coffee, tea, sugar, and also the coconut oil and spices intended for the curry were kept. He also carried 25 pounds of rice. Our hundred rockets, the mats on which we would sleep and eat, and a few round pillows was the cargo of the ninth. The clothes of my friend Templijn and mine (we were taking only the bare necessity) were carried with a few other small things by the tenth man. The slave boy of d'Allemand was our cymbalist and also carried a leather bag with our ammunition, gunpowder, bullets, and filled cartouches. The boy of the cooper had to beat the other cymbal and he also cook during the trip.

Baker George

The aforementioned d'Allemand was probably a French spy who was arrested on arrival in Colombo, but evidence of this I have not been able to find. Also George, the former baker of Nagapatnam, joined the group. Haafner had his reservations about this deaf alcoholic soldier from Strasbourg.

> I was not very happy about this travel companion, because George had two major defects which made him in my opinion completely unsuitable for our journey. For he was deaf, and on top of that, almost constantly drunk. Aside from that, he was a nice guy who was always cheerful and pleasant despite the miserable state in which he found himself. He was a great lover

Fig. 10 From *Reize te voet door het Eiland Ceilon* (Amsterdam 1810). A Singhalese Chieftain.

of everything that can be called spirits. He chatted continuously and had the most ridiculously comical face that one could imagine. Otherwise, he was big and strong and he definitely didn't lack courage.

I knew him from Nagapatnam where he was a soldier in the service of the VOC and also ran a bakery. He had been born in Strasbourg, where he also had been a baker. A series of miraculous events and incidents were the reason why he was now here in Jaffna, where he was kept alive by charity.

He had often expressed the wish to go to Colombo to start a bakery there, because he was indeed a good baker and a skillful and experienced cook. If he had not been attracted to the bottle so much he would have had a comfortable life.

Although as I said I had little interest in him as a traveling companion, I let myself be persuaded by chief Templijn. He told me that we would not give George more arak or spirits than we wanted and that his deafness would not prevent him to help us if we would be attacked by a wild animal.

Haafner and Templijn had planned a trip along the west coast that would take them through Kalmunai, Pooneryn, Pallavarayankaddu, Vidattaitivu, Mantota, Vankalai, Arippu, Puttalam, Chilaw, Madampe, Marawila, and Negombo to Colombo: a tour of 250 kilometers as the crow flies which would take three weeks. The company departed June 9 and arrived on July 3, 1783.

We four Europeans looked like a gang of robbers who went on the expedition. Chief Templijn, d'Allemand and I had each a long hunting knife, two-edged at the end, a pair of pistols in our belts, a bandoleer on the belly and a shotgun over our shoulder. The deaf baker was armed with a large hussar's saber which dragged onto the ground.

Already on the first evening, yet again under the influence of too much alcohol, George told his story.

When he conjured in his mind's eye the tender farewell between Anna and me and the tears she shed, he said with a sneer on his face: In truth! Sir! If you knew the women just as well as I, if they had teased, beaten, chased and ruined you as they did me, you would not pay as much attention to them, much less to her crocodile tears. Because I'm talking still, he continued, and have no mood for sleeping, to pass the time I need to tell you something of my life. Especially about women and all the disasters and accidents that they have caused me. Alas! They are the cause that I am now doomed to wander around as a wretched beggar and lead a disastrous, miserable and poor life. I leave it to your judgment whether I haven't got all possible reason to curse and detest this false treacherous, inconstant and faithless gender.

After this introduction, he began to tell his life, all the time punctuated by reproaches at and insults against women. Because he spoke a mixture of broken Dutch and High German, lavishly laced with cursing and with the accent of Strasbourg, framing his story with ridiculous gestures and facial expressions that made him even less good-looking, it was not possible to hear him without constantly bursting with laughter.

He was married to four women in different cities in Europe. As far as he knew they were all still alive when he left for the East but they knew nothing of each other's existence. They had done all the torments to him ever to be afflicted on a man by evil and angry women. The marital problems he recounted at length were indeed remarkable and funny.

He had to leave his first wife because he feared for his life. She was a devil in human guise. The second had sold him to a Prussian pressganger and as a result he had lost his hearing in the Battle of Rosbach. The third squandered all his money, drank like a sailor, and left him to be a pauper. The fourth, whom he had married in Hamburg sold him to a Dutch kidnapper and that was how he had landed as a soldier in Nagapatnam. There he had started a bakery, and that would definitely have been a success if he hadn't been drinking so much. Which he did to forget his domestic woes, as is a common excuse. Here he had married his fifth wife, a black Roman Catholic girl from the pariah caste. She was a pretty thing and worked as a maid for a European woman named Barbara, who ran a coffee bar. He had become enmeshed with her and encouraged by Barbara he committed the folly of marrying the girl.

A few days after his wedding, I accidentally passed by his house with some friends. We stepped inside to see how things stood with the young married couple. We reeled from one surprise to another when we saw the door was open and it was completely empty. Nobody, no furniture, no baking tools, there was nothing. We went to Barbara, who lived not far from there, and asked if George had moved. She told us that he had been taken to the hospital the previous day where he was in critical condition. About Doortje, his wife, she knew nothing. Driven by curiosity, I visited him some time later in hospital. There I found him in a pitiable condition. He was in the midst of a terrible cure that he had to take to free him from the poison that Doortje had administered to him.

That George was pig-headed when it came to women would be demonstrated later in Colombo.

Most Reasonable of the Unreasonable

In the time that Haafner was in Sri Lanka, the elephant population had increased dramatically due to war, as the capture of elephants had come to a standstill. Elephants created major damage in the villages when they passed through. Even now, in the north of Sri Lanka there is great awe for these animals. The villagers try to scare the elephants by hanging large drawings of people from their stilt houses. At night fires were lighted with the same purpose. An elephant troop passed the camp where Haafner and his companions spent the night. The nature that Haafner found so attractive by day, instilled fear in him at night. The one could not exist without the other in the sublime world that was Haafner's:

> It is no longer the vast forest that echoes with the gay and confused voices of birds in the morning. Despite the dense foliage the sun's rays spread a charming twilight through the forest, but in the evening they make way for utter darkness. A deathly silence replaces the singing with which the feathered forest dwellers greeted the bygone day at its birth. Occasionally one hears only the mournful tones of the night owl that reverberate with a terrible echo and fill the soul with misery. Then the roar and continuous howling of jackals, tigers, and other wild animals, which can be heard at various distances, is suddenly replaced by an ominous silence.
>
> One hears the crash of young trees and branches uprooted and jerked by elephants, which feed on their fruits and leaves. Suddenly a terrible noise approaches. One hears cracking and snapping as though half a city is being consumed by raging flames. It hisses like a hurricane in the tops of the trees, the

ground rumbles as if hit by an earthquake, and a continuous roaring sound like that of a large quantity of trumpets seems to be the sign of an attack. In a word, it is a troop of several hundred elephants that move to another part of the forest after they have eaten bare their previous residence. With a tight trot and joined forces they make their way through the dense forest, and they fling and trample everything in their way except large, thick trees. It is impossible to give an accurate picture of the noise and crackling that is caused by the rupturing and splitting of hundreds of trees. Still, you can get an idea when you imagine the sound of a great big tree snapped in half like a thin twig in a split second with an enormous strength. If you compare that with the amount of trees that are simultaneously and continuously snapped by a troop of elephants that tread a wide path through the jungle, then you can have an idea. Add to this the drone of the soil which is caused by the running of many elephants—even one elephant makes the earth tremble—and it is accompanied by the sound of many trumpets, only then you can form a faint idea of this indescribable and terrifying noise.

In his description of Ceylon, Haafner shows much sympathy for the elephant whom he calls "the most reasonable of the unreasonable". He felt less affinity with bears. The ones common in Sri Lanka are much smaller than the European brown bear. They have extremely long claws which they use for defense. In Sri Lanka there are still many people whose faces bare an impression of an encounter with a bear. Haafner too almost brought back such a souvenir from Ceylon. Occasionally the coastal road diverted inland and led through the woods:

The path we followed and which, according to me, went southeastwards, was so narrow that we could only walk in a train. Such paths run here and there through the dense forests, and some cross the whole island. There are three or four going all the way to Kandy which is centrally located on the island. The remarkable thing about these paths are the two-men-high hedges on either side. They are so steep, going straight up, and so smooth and dense that you might think they have been planted by human hands and pruned and trimmed by an experienced gardener.

We had only followed the path for a quarter of an hour, when I experienced something which almost would have made an end to my life and travels.

The path was, as I said, very narrow. We had to walk in single file like a troupe of wild geese. D'Allemand and I walked ahead. We were engaged in a deep conversation when suddenly a bear of extraordinary size shot from the hedge right in front of us to cross the path. The dense hedge had prevented him from seeing us and he had not smelled us because of his speed.

The unexpected closeness of this monster that stood before me and seemed undecided whether he would attack me or retrace his steps stopped me from jumping backwards. I had hardly seen him, and before I knew it, I fell in front of him on the ground. Because the path here was too narrow to walk in pairs next to each other, we had to move obliquely. Therefore d'Allemand found himself one step behind me at the appearance of the bear, which gave him the time to make his escape.

I wanted, just as I had fallen, to get up immediately to flee or to defend myself. But before I had the time, I saw that the bear, standing in front of me with terrible rumbling and growling, was about to attack me with raised claws. I had only partly stood up when I saw this and froze. Hence I could absolutely not move. Nothing could be done now, because the slightest movement of me or the others would have meant that the bear would have hit me with his claws, which he held just above my head. He seemed to gather all his power to mete out a direct blow. I already surrendered my soul to God and waited for death with eyes closed. At this decisive moment I heard something whistle past my ears. The shot which fell at the same moment scared the bear so much that he, instead of attacking me, uttered an awful howl and fled through the same opening in the woods from which he had come.

Rarely have I been so close to the end of my life. Not only because of the bear, who, had he given me a blow with his paws in which they have an incredible amount of strength, could have cleaved my head, but also because I could have been killed by the bullet, which d'Allemand had shot with a trembling hand and which I heard whistle past my ears. This pistol shot, however, saved my life. Although my travel companions and the coolies who walked some paces behind us made ready to come to my rescue, it wouldn't have helped much, and the bear would have certainly struck. The bear was fortunately not affected by the shot because in that case he would have torn me apart in his rage.

Fig. 11 From *Reize te voet door het Eiland Ceilon* (Amsterdam 1810). Haafner's life is saved by a travel companion who shoots a bear in the woods of Ceylon.

Mestizo among the *Mestizos*

After that incident they continued their journey and arrived in Vidattaltivu, a town on the Mannar coast. Already in his description of his way of life in Sadras, Haafner expresses his love for life in an intercultural society. The acculturation or integration process through which Haafner increasingly started to feel a part of indigenous society, proceeded. He enjoyed engaging with the local population and was proud that he was considered one of them. Often he makes mention of this in his time in Sadras:

> The Bramin seemed very pleased that he had found someone with whom he could speak in his own language.

It was not restricted to speaking the language but also in his behavior and appearance. Haafner looked more and more like a local.

> I laughed by myself that this good man mistook me for a *mestizo*.
> True, I had the whole manner and appearance. He deceived

himself only partially because in addition to walking without shoes and socks, my face was sunburned and I spoke Tamil fluently and purely.

A lot of the lower VOC staff dissolved over time almost entirely into the local population. Why would soldiers go back to cloudy Holland, where they led a slave existence, while in the tropics with its permissiveness and abundance of fruit and meat they lacked nothing? They lived in a constant intoxication that was never disturbed by arrogant governors, sanctimonious preachers, or rectilinear do-gooders. Haafner offers a good illustration of this in the Voet family, who had then already lived for three generations in the village of Vidattaltivu.

We followed the sergeant to his hut and met a large company. It consisted of four young girls, three *mestizo* women with their husbands sitting under a large tamarind tree in front of the door and entertaining themselves with the sound of an Indian zither embellishing their voices. The sergeant told us that he gave a family party on the occasion of his daughter's visit. She was married to a youngster from Mannar the previous week. He introduced his wife, his sister and husband, his two daughters, and those of his brother.

They immediately served a kind of strong arak distilled of palm wine and the bark of a tree. The bark gave an unpleasant smell to the drink that I cannot compare better than with the stench of bedbugs. We dared not refuse the disgusting drink, and even less did we want them to drink our beverages. If they would have had the slightest suspicion that we were provided with good wine and liqueurs, there would certainly not have been a drop left. After this dinner was served. That brought our stomach, which was quite upset by the great intake of the disgusting liquor, a bit back to normal. The meal consisted of rice and excellent game. Everyone had his plate on his knees, and we ate with great gusto. During dinner our friendly innkeeper told us that he was only a corporal with the pay of a sergeant, with six Topass soldiers under his command and that his work consisted only of monitoring a few salt pans that were situated before the village and the collection of fees and taxes for the VOC. He further said that Vidattaltivu fell under the jurisdiction of Jaffnapatnam, and that he was called Jan Voet, and that his father and grandfather had spent their entire lives on this post. He said, further, that he was a *mestizo* and an avid hunter. He

Fig. 12 From *Reize in eenen Palanquin*, vol. 1 (Amsterdam 1808). *Mestizo* women on their way to church in Jakarta, around 1772.

narrated this with such a childish chattiness and good sense that
I could not but secretly envy this man. It did not occur to Voet
that he was actually banished to a place where his ancestors were
already buried and who were not, like me, chased around the
world by an unwholesome desire.

An important part of the relaxed lifestyle in the tropics were the animated
parties that were celebrated at the slightest provocation. This applied to the
Voet family as well:

> As soon we had finished supper the zither was taken up again.
> D'Allemand who enjoyed this kind of music, secretly instructed
> his slave to surprise the party with his violin. Hardly the sound
> of this instrument had struck their ears when they looked like
> struck by electrical fire. Everybody got up and the young girls,
> encouraged by the example of their parents, requested a contra
> dance. We sputtered that we were too tired, but in spite of that
> they took us by the hand and pulled us in line. Everyone, even
> the old corporal and his wife, wanted to dance. It made one
> erupt with laughter to see the jumps and grimaces made from
> joy by the exuberant baker. I would wish the reader, even if only
> once, could have the delight of seeing his comic face to get an
> idea of the bizarre way in which he not only pulled his face but
> moved his whole body.
>
> After having danced for some time we could no longer carry
> on because of our tiredness, and we sat down before the hut.
> The rest of the company now also satisfied, joined us and started
> to sing Malabar love songs. I excelled in singing these songs, and
> the whole party joined in with me. My travel companions who
> couldn't understand a word and certainly could not sing them,
> looked at me with astonishment. From that time I rose to high
> esteem with our coolies who were listening at some distance.

Haafner was flattered when the locals respected him when he demonstrated
his interest in their culture and language. In his *Travels on Foot through the Island
of Ceylon* he shows this by including a comparative list of Dutch, Sinhalese,
and Tamil words. He noted that from Puttalam onward only Sinhalese and
no more Tamil was spoken. From Vidattaltivu they continued their trip via
Negombo to Colombo, where they arrived in early July 1783. About the
capital of the VOC in Ceylon Haafner says little. The capitals of the colonial
authority did not appeal to him. After two weeks chief Templijn found that

the vacancy of master cooper had already been filled. He wanted to get back to Jaffnapatnam as soon as possible. Baker George remained in Colombo, as he was about to marry for the sixth time!

Fig. 13 From *Lotgevallen op eene reize van Madras over Tranquebar naar het Eiland Ceilon* (Haarlem 1806). Jacob Haafner negotiating with a representative of Hyder Ali Khan, around 1780.

Haafner and Templijn left again towards Jaffnapatnam in mid-July and were accompanied by a Portuguese Tomasio de Cruz, who claimed he knew where a great treasure was hidden in the mountains. In the beginning Haafner gave little attention to his stories, but as the return journey proceeded, his sense of adventure and his passion to see Kandy began to surface. Eventually he let himself be persuaded and trekked inland with de Cruz. Probably this part of his narrative, in contrast to the journey to Colombo, is more fantasy than not. It gave him the opportunity to elaborate on the dangers of the jungle. Yet it is not entirely impossible that he based his narrative on his own experience. In a manuscript on how the Hindus thought about punishments after death which he sent in 1797— before he got the idea to put his journey across Ceylon into writing—to the Hollandsche Maatschappij der Wetenschappen (the Dutch Society of Sciences) he says:

But on my journey through the inner part of this island [Ceylon], when I strayed from my companions, and wandered alone in the middle of this terrible and lonely wildernesses for five days and nights, I heard in one of these nights a howling, as that of some people being tortured or beaten.

Hereafter follows a description of those sounds, which is later included in his travelogue.

Delusion and *Pimberah*

It was about midnight when I was suddenly startled out of my sad reverie by a sound like that of the barking of dogs. It was occasionally accompanied by dull and hollow tones that seemed to come from the mountain which raised up on the other side of the watercourse. Before I could make out what the sound was, it emerged far behind me. I thought I clearly heard the voices of several persons laughing loudly. This was in indescribable contrast with the quiet of the night and the previous solitude and deathly silence of the place. The noise continued for some minutes and seemed to quickly come closer, and again to suddenly move away. I stood up from my seating. An unexpected shiver ran through all my limbs, and I listened with a heart beating with fear. From the remote distance the barking sounded fast through the deep silence of the night and was answered by the echoes of the neighboring rocks. Now again an eerie silence prevailed around me. Suddenly I clearly heard from behind the rock where I stood a nasty scream. The blood ran cold in my veins. I could no longer control myself. I had to see what it was, I said to myself, even if it were the devil himself. I armed myself with a big stone and hurled myself half desperately from the cave where I was hiding. At the same moment I heard behind a rock ten paces away from me such a mixture of strange tones, of a vile pitch, penetrating, atrocious and unheard, that I put my fingers in my ears. I was imbued with shuddering and terror and fatally affected by this infernal noise. With flying haste I rushed back to the cave, and as a result I bashed my head against a projection of the cave and nearly ripped open my skull. The blood was pouring down my face, and I withdrew, trembling like a leaf, in the far corner of the cave.

Fig. 14 From *Reize te voet door het Eiland Ceilon* (Amsterdam 1810). Jacob Haafner is attacked by a giant snake in Ceylon, around 1780.

Haafner first didn't want to tell the story to anybody, but he overcame his embarrassment and found out he was not the only one to hear such voices. The Sinhalese attributed them to evil spirits, and Europeans called them forest devils. These may have been imaginary, but the *pimberah*, as Haafner called the giant python he was to encounter next wasn't at all. Haafner was completely lost in the woods.

> I heard a terrifying hissing and saw something large move in a thick tree. As fast as possible as the fear that gripped me allowed, I fled to a rock where I arrived, out of breath. I realized that I could not get on top of it, and out of desperation I decided to retrace my steps to the watercourse. That act of desperation seemed to me at that moment the best thing I could do and the only course that remained in my sad state.
>
> Not considering the hazard, fatigue, and predicament that I was about to experience, I picked up my rifle and pack that I had dropped when I suddenly heard the same hissing which had made

me flee in great hurry from the woods. I looked around and saw a monstrous serpent of gigantic size slowly slip out of the wood through the opening from which I had just fled. The snake cut me off completely. When I saw the snake it seemed as if the earth opened beneath my feet. I uttered a terrible shriek. From terror and astonishment I did not know what to do. I lost in one swoop both courage and hope. My confused and dizzy mind wandered around without it being able to fix on any one object. I stood as if struck by lightning and did not know what to do in this perilous and dangerous situation. Where to flee to? Where could I hide myself? I saw the horrible monster getting ready to swallow me. I saw his glinting eyes and neck swollen with anger.

He cut me off my path completely, and I could do nothing but throw myself into the watercourse which was to my left. Before me was the steep rock wall, and to my right an impenetrable web of vine and tendrils which took away the hope to escape along that side. What a plight, great God! You must have found yourself in a similar circumstance to imagine the horror. An overwhelming indecision held me in its grip but when I saw the horrible monster, only a hundred paces away from me, increase his speed, and open his jaws to engulf me, I threw myself out of sheer desperation against the rock at the place where it hung over the waterway. I jumped more than a meter into the air and managed to get a hold of a crack in the rock. Without the threat I would never have been able to make such a leap, because it gave me the strength and the skill to make it. I was hovering above the abyss for a few seconds before I could put my feet on a more or less flat spot and free myself of the weight of my body. During this fearful struggle I called upon God from the bottom of my heart because every moment I feared to be caught and devoured by the monster chasing me. Fortunately, he was not of the kind that crawls on his tail with raised body such as the cobra. I did my best to save my life. By clinging to every bulge and crack, I managed to grab the edge of the rock, and hoist myself upwards.

Forsaken by Anna

Not long after this encounter with the *pimberah* Haafner returned safely to Jaffnapatnam and lost himself once again in the arms of Anna. Also, in his own words, his financial position was improved considerably since his investments in his friends' businesses had done well. He therefore looked assured of an independent life, and he was about to marry Anna. However, a few days after his return, he found himself compelled to travel again, to settle some financial issues in Nagapatnam. Upon his arrival there, he discovered that his business and that of his partners had been confiscated through extortions by officials, and he owned almost nothing anymore. Haafner was not unhappy, because he was still able to support himself by his garden in Jaffnapatnam, and he could still build a living with Anna.

Bad news travels fast: just before he was ready to start the return journey, Haafner received a letter from Anna which distressed him. It said that she had heard that he had lost his capital and no longer wanted to impose herself on him. She would join her mother in Goa. Haafner still did not want to believe he was abandoned and returned to Jaffnapatnam. There, Templijn told him that she was not in Goa, but had rather run off with a wealthy diamond merchant when she had heard of Haafner's misfortune. Haafner fell into a depressive mood.

> Poor, without prospects, abandoned by her who was most valuable to me, my life became a heavy burden and more than once I was about to end it.

That did not happen and Haafner decided to try his luck again in mainland India.

Chapter 4

Passion for India

Haafner sold his possessions and embarked for the Danish settlement of Tranquebar on the Coromandel Coast. There missionaries offered him to let him become a teacher. Haafner found their offer outrageous; besides, he had a profound aversion against the teaching profession.

> I've always had an unconquerable aversion for the profession of teacher. I equated the existence of the person who had the misfortune to be doomed to such a miserable and ungrateful profession with that of the slave.

Soon he was on a boat to Madras, where he asked de Souza if he could arrange his passage to Calcutta because he wanted to try his luck in that city. De Souza, however, was still in need of accountants, and wanted to employ him. Haafner rejected this because he did not feel at ease in Madras. There were several reasons for this. Haafner feared that someone would find out about those letters he was meant to deliver to an English general but which he had given to the French. If this was discovered, Haafner would be hanged without mercy. Moreover, the city was saturated with memories of the famine and Anna.

> In every street loomed before my mind the piles of corpses and dying that had succumbed to hunger (...) These thoughts, which I could not banish from my mind, brought back in my memory by every street and every square, made me abhor this city and its inhuman residents. Worse even than this was my unhappy love, which made staying in Madras unbearable. I tried to distance myself from that love and everything that reminded me of it, but with every step I took Madras continuously called up images in me that reminded me of my lost happiness. The

house where we lived, the pond in which we bathed, our favorite woods and hiking trails, even the spot on the beach where we said goodbye when she left for Tranquebar, everything called up bitter memories and tore my soul with jealousy, anger, remorse, sadness, and a thousand distressing emotions I could not keep under control.

In short Haafner came to the conclusion that he had to leave Madras even though he could get a good job there. He embarked for Calcutta, arriving two weeks later.

But that was not the only, nor has it been the last, time that my—if one wants to call it romantic or fanciful—thinking stood in the way of my career. Happy is he who is not so sensitive. He may not know the titillating delights that are evoked by sensitivity, but he is spared all the grievous affections to which susceptible people are exposed continuously. There I stood in the middle of Calcutta, devoid of friends and acquaintances, left to my fate, and with a shrinking money supply. I did not know what to do or what would become of me once the little money I had left was finished. The more I thought about my condition, the more acute the concern about the fate that awaited me.

Merchant in Calcutta

In contrast to Madras, where the Europeans were in direct contact with the local population, in Calcutta, which had gradually eclipsed Batavia as the European metropolis in Asia, relations with the local population, except for domestic staff, were minimal. In everything Calcutta looked like a European city—except for the death rates of Europeans, which were still much higher than in their native continent. Haafner finds the town:

The most beautiful in India, with the most formidable fortress outside Europe and buildings surrounded with imposing columns that resemble Greek temples.

He will not be blinded by the dazzle of power and makes his readers aware of what made possible the construction of the city:

A greatness founded on the ruins of the happiness and prosperity of all their neighboring nations and by the blood of millions of innocents, obtained from the robbery of all brought together.

Fig. 15 From *Reize naar Bengalen en terugreize naar Europa* (Amsterdam 1822). Two Bengali types: the Chobdar or staff-bearer and the Peon or messenger.

On January 22, 1784 Haafner witnessed the big celebration on the occasion of the peace between the European powers. That day marked the beginning of an essentially unstoppable British expansion in India and the transition from the "emporialistic" to the imperialistic era. In short: the rise of that totalitarian state. Haafner was at that moment already employed by Joseph Fowke, the former governor of Benares. While Fowke is known in the literature as a grumpy man, he was for Haafner a guardian angel. In the two years that he worked for him, Haafner came to regard Fowke as a father figure. Because of Fowke, Haafner entered into the heart of social life in Calcutta, which largely revolved around music evenings at the houses of wealthy families; and those at the Fowkes' not the least among them. Fowke wrote on February 26, 1784 to his son, Francis, his father's successor as governor:

> Haffner has balanced my books and pronounces that I must have a trifle more than sufficient to discharge all my debts, except the play debt in England—which I gave you account of.

He went on:

> May I now venture to insuring you that Mr. Hastings has determined to resign (...) I believe he wishes to get away as fast as he can.

Fowkes' statement must be read against the background of the conflict between enlightened company employees as Governor General Hastings and the scholar Sir William Jones, who were proponents of close contacts with the academic upper class of the Indian population, and opponents thereof, to which Joseph and Francis Fowke belonged. With a view to the study of Indian culture Hastings and Jones had founded the Asiatick Society, later the Asiatic Society of Bengal, in 1784.

That Haafner would have met Jones and other members of the Asiatick Society should not be excluded. He was, however, not a member of this exclusive society, and there are no contributions by him included in *Asiatick Researches*, the journal of the Society. For the assertion that he translated a manuscript from Tamil to English for Jones no hard evidence has been found. But he knew the contents of the article by the architect Sir William Chambers on the seven temples of Mahabalipuram which was published in the first issue of *Asiatick Researches* in 1788, according to an English review in *The Quarterly Review* in 1812, in which Haafner is accused of plagiarism. The similarities in text are indeed striking, but can't the accusation of plagiarism which the reviewer voices towards Haafner not be reversed? Is it not possible that Chambers copied a text by Haafner which he made for Jones about Tamil Nadu, which has been lost?

Whereas the interest of Jones was directed to science, the Fowkeses were more interested in partying and Indian musicians and dancers. Haafner wrote in mid-November 1785 to Francis Fowke:

> Mr. Fowke has engaged Vincent to go with him to Benares (. . .)
> He has found him the soundest and best musician in India and far superior to Mr. Kidd Mea, and others of that class, So that he will be a valuable acquisition to you.

Joseph Fowke gave almost weekly dinner dances. Haafner reports:

> The urge to dance has grown to a complete craze with European women. The consequence is that most die of the pleurisy or inflammations before their time.

Virtually every day there was a feast organized by Westerners for which astronomically high entrance fees were charged. Except for food, everything was extremely expensive in Calcutta. A receipt for the rent of his house, in the name of "James Haffner", shows that Haafner had to pay the equivalent of 60 guilders a month for the rent of his house. This was double of what he earned in a month with the Dutch East India Company at the end of his career. Haafner's living standards must have substantially increased, if he was able to sustain such a lifestyle.

That was because Haafner had managed to start trading himself. This is evident in a letter from Joseph Fowke to Francis: "Haffner has been absent on some business of his own these two days." That Haafner traded is further evident from letters addressed to him in Hindi from Bengal businessmen related to the sale of a batch of lime. In Calcutta, Haafner thus gathered the capital that enabled him to live carefree for some years after returning to Europe. He was apparently also well acquainted with the diamond trade, as he arranged the transactions for Francis Fowke. These consisted of lots of diamonds, bulses, which were given to captains of vessels and then sold through trading houses in London, on which drafts were then drawn. He writes about this to Francis:

> This serves you [Francis] to inform you that your bulses [. . .] have been duly deliver'd into the hands of the captains.

Fowke sent Haafner on missions regularly, including one to Chinsurah, a town which lay upstream on the Hooghly and which had been an important trading place in the heyday of the VOC. There Haafner came face to face with a cremation.

> I had only just a look at the corpse when I thought it was moving. I was shocked terribly when I saw how the corpse slowly erected itself between the flames and saw it stare at me with the most horrible gestures and frightening looks, while in an indescribably ghastly way, it seemed, it made futile attempts to open its mouth.
>
> Transfixed by this unexpected and gruesome spectacle of horror and stunned with fright I remained standing motionless with eyes fixed on the ghost. I could not move or shape thoughts of what I saw. Suddenly I heard a noise behind me and I looked around with fright. It was, as far as I could see it in the light of the fire through the bushes, a local slowly approaching with a jar on his head. When he saw me he seemed not less anxious than I was. At that moment the body fell back into the flames, immediately my ridiculous fear disappeared, and I came to my senses. I remembered that the bizarre convulsions of the corpse are caused by the shrinking of the nerves by fire.

Despite this dismal spectacle, Haafner became a declared supporter of cremation instead of burial and being eaten by worms. He rightly saw church burial in Europe as a root cause of many diseases.

The Impetuous Julius Soubise

In addition to interest in indigenous culture and ways of life, Haafner sure had an eye for the inhabitants of the empire, as we have already seen in his description of baker George. He pays much attention to his meeting with Julius Soubise (1754–98). Soubise was sent to India in 1777 by his patroness Catherine Hyde, the Duchess of Queensbury, after he had been amorous with one of the maids of the Duchess. It was the straw that broke the camel's back, as Julius was already known as a great womanizer and spendthrift.

At ten years of age he had been brought from St. Kitts to London and taken under the wing of the Duchess, who saw to his education. He was not the only black person in London by far. In the second half of the eighteenth century, almost 20,000 freed slaves lived there and had a culture of their own. Recent genetic research in England shows that in the southern half of the country 10 per cent of the population descends from West Indians. While

Soubise drew attention in Calcutta just as he had in London, very little is known about his stay in India. The curious Haafner went to visit him, and so a small portion of the veil is raised.

> Through my friend Diehle I came to know an extraordinary man. He was a Caribbean-born negro slave named Soubise. He was taken to England where he attracted a lot of attention. Catherine Hyde, Duchess of Queensbury, was so taken in with his witty and cheerful comportment she did not rest until she procured Julius. One day while he was serving his mistress, a lady came to visit who was possessed with the ingrained prejudices of whites against the Negro: that he only has the appearance of a man but really is not much more than a reasonless animal. That lady had therefore little appreciation when the Duchess was full of praise for Soubise's intelligence and good manners. She insisted that a black is a stupid creature not capable of abstract knowledge but who has just enough discernment to carry out the simplest daily activities. The Duchess stated the black had the same mental abilities as the European; the black just had to be taught some civilization. The duchess even went as far as to claim that the black rose in natural disposition of mind, intelligence, and comprehension above the Europeans just as he does in strength and agility in the physical areas.

> To prove she was right, the education of the young Soubise was given the utmost attention. Nothing was left from shaping him into a perfect gentleman and she let him be taught along with her son in all the arts and sciences in which he had an interest or aptitude for. It was not long before her efforts were richly rewarded, because soon he surpassed not only her son but also herself, and in a short time he was widely praised for his great general knowledge.

> Vanity played a major role with the Duchess, and it persuaded her to send him to Eton, where he could entertain in a grand state. There he completed his studies just before her death. She left him a pension which enabled him to go on living as before. The fast flowing blood of the African was not able to withstand the temptation and affluence. It was not long before he ran into bad company, led a dissolute life, and got into debt. He sold the annuity to come out of prison in that way.

Fig. 16   From *Reize naar Bengalen en terugreize naar Europa* (Amsterdam 1822). Calcutta
seen from the Hooghly River, around 1785.

But he lived long of the money he amply earned with
teaching Latin, French, music, and dancing. He even founded
a sort of academy for the art of balancing and walking the
tightrope as well as a riding and fencing school. It may seem
unlikely, but he had mastered all those arts and sciences. In some
of them, such as music and horsemanship, he even excelled to a
high degree. He has been famous in London and Calcutta, and
there are many witnesses to his extraordinary abilities. Therefore
I do not have to fear that I may be accused of exaggeration.

Eventually he was forced by debt to flee England when an
opportunity arose to go to India, even though he had earned a
lot of money and counted among his pupils the most significant
people. In India, he almost instantly became overseer of the
stables of the Nabob of Oudeh a post he soon left for Calcutta,
where he could spend the considerable amount of money he
had earned.

His wealth, however, could not last long. He kept a whole
seraglio of women with whom he had several children, all
of whom he had to maintain. Besides, he had a noble and
generous character. He gave or lent money to all his friends and

acquaintances. These were mostly idlers, but at the same time many were people effected by real setbacks who thanked him for their preservation and that of their families. I always found it difficult to say goodbye to him. He was not only very civilized, but also an inexhaustible source of witticisms that was perfectly suited to cheer a melancholy and wistful mind. Always busy and content, he considered life only from the positive side, and he never lost his good humor and nonchalance, even in the most awkward circumstances that he was often in.

Poor Soubise was, shortly after I had met him, in the prison from which he had already escaped so often. He had landed up there because of his affair with a certain Miss Rose. She was a very handsome *mestiza* of French descent, as white as a European woman. Miss Rose was maintained by an Englishman. Soubise, who lived close to his house, had often spied on her while she was smoking her pipe on the flat roof of the house. In this way he came into contact with her. That was to cost him dearly. She was given 300 rupees monthly by the Englishman but she spend at least two times as much with gambling, buying clothes, and so on. To cover those expenses, she tried to lure everyone into her net that she thought might be able to contribute to her craving for wealth and spending. She knew the intricacies of seduction and because she was a very amiable woman, it took her no effort to ruin several people, including the poor Soubise.

He told us this when I went with a few friends to visit him in the debtors' prison on a certain afternoon, a large isolated building outside the city. We found him in his room in the company of other debtors. They were in a very good mood and spent their time with the finishing of a few bottles of Madeira. They did not seem in the least anxious about their condition, in which one would easily be bored to death.

Haafner's visit to Soubise happened at the end of his two-year stay in Calcutta. According to Haafner, Joseph Fowke even asked him to become partner in the business, but that never came to pass. That plan was thwarted by Francis, who was annoyed at the apparent influence Haafner had on his father; he felt that Jacob had better leave. Haafner probably realized that his position had become untenable. He thought the better of it and left for the Coromandel Coast with a ship full of merchandise at the end of 1786, during an absence of Joseph Fowke. Upon returning Fowke wrote to his son: "Haffner has gone to the coast in my absence without giving me warning." Haafner claims that he had been given the goods as a gift by Fowke.

Before arriving in Bimilipatnam he had the first attack of angina pectoris, a condition that he would eventually die from.

> I just lay in bed when I suddenly felt a sharp pain in my chest. My heart squeezed together, and I could breathe only with great difficulty and was in danger of choking. In this life-threatening condition, I remained completely conscious and fully realized the precariousness of my situation if I did not get help. I tried to call for help, but I could not utter a word or sound. I had just enough strength to get out of my bed and cabin and reached the deck where I collapsed while pointing to my heart. My swollen face, black-blue colour, opened mouth, and vain attempts to breathe caused an onrush of crew and caused utter confusion and consternation. After they had me sniff vinegar and smelling salts, I could again take some air and began to breathe more freely, but an indescribable pressure and pain in my heart area remained.

Haafner didn't let it discourage him. He sold part of his goods and decided to trek with a palanquin further south along the Coromandel Coast.

Sunrise

Haafner's *Reize in eenen Palanquin* (*Travels in a Palanquin*) was published in two parts in 1808, and should be seen as Haafner's *chef-d'œuvre*. In it, his romance with the Indian dancer Mamia is described. The work finally established his name as an author not only in the Netherlands but also abroad because translations into German and French appeared soon after the book was released. What follows is a brief impression of a travelogue which can do no justice to the original, which is much richer in striking observations about culture, customs, and people along the coast of Odisha and Coromandel than can be excerpted here.

The first part of the journey took Haafner from Bimilipatnam to Masulipatnam, a journey of three weeks and almost 300 kilometers through mountains and plains. He hired a cook and ten bearers who took care of his transportation by palanquin. Haafner thought traveling by palanquin was much more comfortable than with a stagecoach in Europe:

> In the whole world there is no easier, safer, and more pleasant means of transportation than a palanquin. Imagine, dear reader,

REIZE

IN EENEN

PALANQUIN;

OF

LOTGEVALLEN EN MERKWAARDIGE
AANTEEKENINGEN OP EENE REIZE
LANGS DE KUSTEN ORIXA
EN CHOROMANDEL.

DOOR

J. HAAFNER.

IN TWEE DEELEN.

EERSTE DEEL.

TE AMSTERDAM BIJ
JOHANNES ALLART,
MDCCCVIII.

Fig. 17 Title page from *Reize in eenen Palanquin*, vol. 1 (Amsterdam 1808).

a machine like a sofa, daybed or couch which is three feet wide and seven feet long. In it one lies on a soft mattress and pillows, as one can lie stretched out on a bed.

Over the crooked bamboo to which this sofa is attached a canopy of green or red material is stretched which offers shelter from the sun (. . .) One can sleep, sit, read, and even write in it. When two palanquins are carried adjacent, the passengers may talk as well as if they are sitting next to each other on a chair. In a word, a palanquin is the most comfortable and entertaining carrying device that has ever been conceived.

That Haafner not only effortlessly adapted to local customs but did this with enthusiasm is demonstrated by the fondness he had developed for bathing:

While the cook was preparing dinner, I went to bathe in the lake. O! how pleasant, how refreshing is such a bath. How it tightens the slackened nerves and fills the heart with courage and the limbs with strength. One feels reborn. All lethargy and melancholy caused by the heat of the day disappears. A tranquility and contentment descends on you which is difficult to describe. The blood flows calmer through the veins, and the pulse beats slower.

Bathing in these hot countries is totally indispensable for health. I had made a habit of it and almost always went at the crack of dawn to a pond to bathe. I shall never forget the fun I enjoyed as the cool water rippled around me while thousands of birds greeted the rising sun, each in their own way, from the overhanging trees and in the bushes nearby. I recommend that anyone who wants to stay healthy in India should take a morning bath and follow as much as possible the way of life of the Indians.

Haafner not only followed, he was deeply interested in it. After a day's journey, he arrived at the mountain Simhachalam where at that time, according to his own words, more than 40,000 people were on pilgrimage to visit a shrine. The main purpose of Haafner's visit was not the shrine but to experience the sublime sunrise, which he could see best from the top of the mountain:

The whole valley was in motion. The roar of the countless crowd was like the roar of a waterfall. Everyone rushed to the mountain. Its crown seemed to be completely on fire from the many torches and wreaths of pitch that were tossed about and spread flames continuously. To this were added rockets that whizzed through the air and formed a bizarre spectacle from the ground.

Full of curiosity and longing I started immediately. I left the headman with the palanquin, took my binoculars, and moved forward in the crowd that rushed in the greatest harmony towards the foot of the mountain.

I kept on going and raced to the top in order to reach it before the sunrise.

Among all those people, I was the only one that ascended the mountain with the intention of seeing from a high vantage point the most beautiful and wonderful sight in nature, the sun rising from the sea. I wanted to be an eyewitness to a phenomenon that more than all the temples and images can let us learn the greatness and omnipotence of the incomprehensible supreme being. Rather than see this amazing spectacle, the veil of which was about to be lifted, everyone was going to attend meaningless and useless ceremonies and ridiculous rituals which like many other church rites don't leave the slightest impression on the soul.

The clamor and bustle at the top of the mountain was indescribable. People's voices, the deafening roar of their wind instruments, the humming of the drums, the clash of cymbals, the whiz of the rockets that were fired everywhere stupefied and surprised me. The whole mountain top was covered with people who were eagerly waiting for the moment that they would carry the deity out of the temple, when the procession would begin.

But I went to the other side of the mountain, a remote and lonely place where no one would bother me, and I could devote myself in silence to my musings and enjoy undisturbed the pleasure I had promised myself. I sat down on a high rock and lit a cigar and watched out with heartfelt longing for the moment when the curtain of the sky would be pulled up.

Without moving my eyes I stared some time into the black night in front of me. Suddenly I saw the sky light up in the east. The sea broke away from the darkness, and the horizon emerged. Gold and purple streaks appeared as struck by a magic hand and fanned out across the eastern horizon. One wave of light after another rolled across the firmament. The stars faded, and soon I bathed in the morning dawn.

Now suddenly long rays shoot like lightning behind the horizon into the heaven. The edge of the sea seethes in fire. From this waving gold the sun rises in glorious majesty. In a state of inexpressible delight, I saw her great disk in glowing splendor before me.

The valley was still covered in darkness, but the peaks of the mountains were already illuminated by light. Slowly that light rolled up the veil that covered the earth and sea, and it was not long before the whole landscape showed itself to me in a thousand hues. High above flew the mountain eagles. They revolved in wide circles and floated around on their spread out wings. They called each other with joy, and their shrill sounds descended on me. Like me they rejoiced in the new day.

What is all the glory and splendor of the kings and great of this world? All their borrowed splendor—how trivial!—How very little!—Compared to this glorious spectacle full of ineffable majesty! To imitate that with human ability is nothing but a sign of their weakness.

The view was endless and fabulous! I wish I had a hundred eyes to encompass it all. I did not know where I was; whether I was alive or if I, liberated from my mortal body, was flying over the heavenly fields. Everything that happened, all the memories of the ups and downs were erased from my soul. Everything was gone from my memory, and I just lived in the present.

Haafner struggled to pry himself away from his ecstatic state of enlightenment. But he had to: his bearers were waiting at the bottom of the mountain.

But this mountain was too special to me. I did not leave without having made a detailed drawing of it.

Haafner must have made a lot of drawings while traveling but to date none have surfaced. From the engravings made on the basis of his drawings, it can be deduced that they must have been very precise.

During the journey Haafner and his companions passed the night usually in a *chauderie*, or cavanserai, a resting place for travelers where everyone could stay for free. In such a *chauderie* near the city of Vizagapatnam (now Visakhpatnam) he met with two fakirs of around 30 and 50 years old doing penance:

Fig. 18 From *Reize in eenen Palanquin*, vol. 1 (Amsterdam 1808). A *chauderie* or traveller's guesthouse near Perla-Chirala, around 1786.

The latter had imposed on himself the terrible and painful penance of always keeping both arms above his head with hands clasped and never bringing them down. This he had sustained.

Great God! Where to do bigotry and superstition lead humanity! What oddities and crimes they make him commit! The two arms of the fakir had withered because of the unnatural position and were so stiff that he could not possibly bring them down anymore or loosen the hands. They caused him now absolutely no more pain but the first year that had been very different because according to him the pain had been beyond description.

He was accompanied by another fakir, who was about thirty, who fed and helped him. He walked around stark naked and had an iron ring through his penis that was as thick as a quill and as big as the palm of one hand, the ends of which were soldered together. He had made the vow of chastity. Knowing that the mind is strong but the flesh is weak, he had wisely armed himself against an insidious attack of the flesh. One must have an iron will to stay emotionless in the presence of young and beautiful women and girls, and in the *chauderie* a few were staying. It would not be a bad idea in my opinion to require anyone who has made such an unnatural vow to wear a ring like his.

It was therefore not the case that Haafner embraced the whole of Indian culture. He remained a judicious observer.

Mamia!

Via Palicol, now Palakollu, but which was, in 1786, one of the few VOC offices left in India, Haafner arrived in Masulipatnam in early April where he stayed for a few weeks to organize his business. In that time this city was known for the most beautiful temple dancers or *devadasis* (from the Sanskrit *devi*, "deity", and *dasi*, "slave"). As a prelude to the second part of the journey, in which his love for one of them is a central theme, Haafner devotes an entire chapter to the *devadasis*. This first accurate description of them in western literature contextualizes the negative and corrupt image that missionaries had given of them. Haafner was particularly impressed with how they looked, especially compared to how women in Europe are dressed. He waxes lyrical:

> Many of them are endowed by nature with a beautiful bosom. To prevent its deformation for as long as possible they enclose each breast in a form attached to each other with straps and tied on the body around the back. Because these forms are very thin, transparent, and are elastic and correspond with their skin colour, it is difficult to distinguish this garment from the body. In short, they take great care to retain their breasts' youthful beauty for as long as possible. They do not allow their breasts to be treated roughly or touched.

In addition to this description of a precursor of the brassiere, Haafner goes into the smallest detail of their jewelry, the use of nail polish, makeup, their tattoos, their bare navel, the fragrant oils with which they anoint themselves, and the garlands with which they are adorned. Haafner concludes:

> A young, beautiful and fully decorated dancer is, with her casual and loose posture and spirited pace, an enchanting and alluring creature. Her simple headdress; the partial baring of the beautiful breasts and rounded arms; the close-fitting dress that with artful neatness and folding is wound around the high

and shapely hips; and the graceful curves of the veil. In one word; the whole dress of these girls is perfectly calculated to accentuate their natural beauty, and add luster to it. The dress shines on their gestures so that every move they make brings out the best of her body. Her entire figure is visible in the most charming and most demure manner.

From Masulipatnam he continues to travel south to Madras with a palanquin and ten bearers. At the end of the first day of the trip they take up residence in the *chauderie* of Perla-Chirala where he meets Mamia, his future beloved, for the first time.

It was almost dark when I arrived in the *chauderie*. I found there already several travelers who were to stay overnight and were stretched tired on their mats or were making their food ready. My friend Captain Huau, who is born in Batavia, was waiting for me with a bowl of punch which he had prepared in my absence. This was our daily evening drink. We carried arak with us, and we bought lime and sugar at the bazaar or in a small shop.

Meanwhile, it became more and more crowded in the *chauderie*. Pilgrims, members of the wandering caste, farmers and craftsmen, soldiers, itinerant merchants with their parcels of merchandise, and others with pack animals flocked inside from all sides. When it was already seven o'clock, the crowd was increased by a troop of itinerant dancers and musicians.

Subsequent to having bathed according to the custom of the land, although it was already dark, in the nearby pond and put on other clothes, the leader of the troupe, which consisted of seven dancers, approached us. After she had first appropriately greeted me, she offered me and Huau each a flower bouquet. She asked permission to dance for us.

All eyes of the travelers who were close to me and heard her request, focused on me. A soft murmur passed through the whole crowd. The desire and passion to see a dance performance could be read from the eyes of the wives and daughters of the wandering caste and those of other castes who were encamped close to me. For their sake I asked the leader to perform a dance after dinner.

No sooner was it known that I had given my consent to the dance when I heard around me the words "noble lord" and the like.

Fig. 19 From *Reize in eenen Palanquin*, vol. 2 (Amsterdam 1808). Depiction of an Indian dancer or *devadasi* (front view). This is most likely a depiction of Haafner's girlfriend Mamia.

Fig. 20 From *Reize in eenen Palanquin*, vol. 2 (Amsterdam 1808). Depiction of an Indian dancer or *devadasi* (rear view). This is most likely a depiction of Haafner's girlfriend Mamia.

Almost the entire *chauderie* was in motion, and the good news spread like wildfire, from traveler to traveler. Those who were sleeping were woken up. All left their sleeping mats and couches to get a good seat in time. Also the villagers arrived *en masse* to attend this entertainment. The *chauderie* was full in no time.

After we had eaten, I informed the dancers that they could start. Room was made. Everyone moved aside and the *lakshmis* (earthen lamps with the image of the goddess of fortune Lakshmi) were placed in niches (in the walls of the *chauderies* everywhere, triangular holes of masonry are constructed in which *lakshmis* were placed and when it was dark, it seemed the *chauderie* was completely illuminated).

When everything was ready, I sat with Huau on the mattress of my palanquin with a fresh bowl of punch in front of us. While we smoked our cigars, we waited with the crowd that formed a wide circle around us for the arrival of the dancers, who soon made their entrance, with their heads covered in veils and accompanied by the musicians.

I gave a sign with my hand, and the first notes sounded. Then I saw the wielder of the cymbals, and at the sound of his instrument the veils fell away, and suddenly before us there are seven young nymphs with shapely figures, bareheaded and fully adorned. Again the cymbals sounded and the nymphs formed a row. With an obeisance they drew near, while placing the right hand on the chest, with which they show their respect, according to custom.

Now the music rises louder, and through the quiet village echo the joyful and clamorous tones of the oboe, trumpet, drum, and a one-string instrument with a monotonous bagpipe drone; and the dance begins.

How fast and free are all the movements of the quick nymphs, how their gestures correspond with their steps, how pleasing and enchanting are the passionate movements of their shapely limbs, and with how much art and skill they unfold before us all their charms, without offending modesty.

After they had danced for about an hour, I signed with my handkerchief they had to stop. The music stopped. I had to compliment them now, as was the custom.

Enough! Beautiful young lady, I said. It's enough for now. You've entertained me greatly by your artful dance and filled my heart with joy. Rambha (the goddess of dance) could not surpass you. If you're not tired, sit by me and delight my ear with your lovely voice.

They welcomed my praise and seemed to be astonished that a European was so well informed on the customs and language of the land. They were immediately willing to accommodate my request.

Mats were brought and they sat down in a semicircle in front of me. Just behind them were the musicians and around at a small distance the crowd that listened silently with the greatest attention.

To their repeated requests to know what kind of romance I wanted to hear, I chose *kami* (love stories). They sang the love story of Bidya, Princess of Bhordowan and Sundar, Prince of Hostinapur. How he was thwarted in his love by a powerful sorceress and chased through countless adventures and incidents eventually achieved the possession of his wonderful Bidya.

It was almost midnight when the singing stopped. They wanted to begin another love story but I refused. I gave the leader of the dancers a tray of betel and areca nuts and money. They stood up and rewarded my courtesy and generosity with many regards and gratitude and said their goodbyes.

Everyone went to bed happy, and Haafner lay in his palanquin.

I was hardly asleep when I was awakened by a movement of the cover. Who is there, I asked as I lifted the cover to see who came to disturb me. It's me, sir! said someone in a very soft tone. It was the chambermaid of the dance troupe. I am bringing you a thousand greetings from the young virgin with the yellow bodice and the wreath of white flowers around her head. Your kindness and affable ways have opened her heart for you like a flower to the rays of the sun. She gives you this leaf of areca nut she prepared herself as evidence of the esteem in which she holds you. She sits at the foot of your couch and is looking forward to your orders.

There was among the troupe of dancers a girl of about fifteen years that was very beautiful in figure and face and who sang very gracefully and artfully.

She had no doubt noticed, while she was singing for me, that I had looked at her with great pleasure and attention. From this

she had probably concluded that I longed to become acquainted
with her in a different way. Therefore she had sent a matchmaker.

Haafner, however, rejected the offer, to the great incomprehension of the
matchmaker.

How, sir! she said, you despise the lovely Mamia! That surprises
me. I seem to have noticed that you were not indifferent to her.
Why have you now closed your heart to her? What do you fear?
She is my foster child, and you are the first to whom she offered
the betel of love.

Haafner, however, was adamant and laughed at her. The next day he was
already sorry that he had rejected her love proposal. He still greeted Mamia
at his departure, but she did not respond. When he looked back after a while
he saw her crying and wondered whether it was real or pretense. He was very
moved by it, and not long after he came to the conclusion that he was head
over heels in love with her.

Snakebite

Haafner continued his journey and arrived in the village of Karraduru
(probably today's Kadavakuduru). He went to gather some dry leaves to light
the fire. Suddenly he felt a sharp pain in the tip of his middle finger of his
right hand. He withdrew his hand and saw a snake hanging from it:

I screamed with terror and dismay and hurled the snake
forcefully off me.

It marked the beginning of a two-week period in which Haafner hovered
between life and death, at least in his later telling of the story. In the original
edition, his struggle with the snake bite takes almost 80 pages; this part of the
work can be seen as a long dramatic preamble which will eventually drive him
into the arms of Mamia. He wanted to get to Madras as quickly as possible
to see his cousin Beisser, a doctor from Colmar. He even traveled at night. At
three days' journey from Madras, he arrived in Nawabpet where he wanted to
visit the temple complex. Given his situation, he wasn't able to, but he gave
his bearers instructions to walk past the temple at a slow pace. That would
afterwards prove to be his rescue.

Just opposite these buildings was a very beautiful pond made of cement
in which there were many people. At the end of it a troupe of women was
bathing.

I took no notice, all my attention was focused on the temple. Then I suddenly heard not far from me the loud shriek of a woman. The voice penetrated deep into my soul because I recognized the voice. I quickly turned. Heaven! It was Mamia, who was bathing with the other dancers in the pond and had just risen up.

My heart trembled with joy. Hold still! Hold still! I shouted to my bearers. Before they had put down the palanquin I had already jumped out. I immediately rushed to her, ignoring and not even realizing what my people and all other people who were bathing or standing there would think of me.

Mamia! I cried very hard, beloved Mamia! At last I see you again. Oh, how often have I thought of you! That was all I could say. Tears came in my eyes and I remained motionless in front of her.

She herself seemed so upset that she did not answer and only laid her hand on her chest and bowed to me.

How pretty she was! Oh, how enchanting! The white muslin cloth was wrapped high under her arms a few times around her body. It clung, still dripping wet, to her graceful and shapely limbs. Clearly I could see her beautiful body in all its charming contours. Her full youthful breasts appeared from under the fine wet linen like the moon from behind a thin shimmering cloud. My senses were totally intoxicated by this unexpected encounter and at the sight of this amiable person, and I was staring at her with open mouth without being able to utter a word.

They agreed to meet later. Haafner's travel companions were amazed that someone who hovered on the verge of death, could recover so miraculously. Soon the matchmaker made her appearance, and Haafner told her that she should arrange a meeting as quickly as possible. Not long after Mamia arrived, and Haafner offered his apologies for returning the love-betel and declared his love for her. She did not blame him but the goddess of fate. Then she told him about her unhappy childhood. She came from a family of healers and doctors. When she was eight years old, her father had married her to a much older friend of his who died shortly after their marriage. She became a widow and was according to Indian customs not allowed to remarry. When her father died four years later, she ended up with a distant relative. It turned out to be an old miser for whom she had to toil day and night. After a year she decided to escape, and was lucky to be picked up by the leader of a dance troupe who trained her to be a dancer in Thanjavur in Tamil Nadu. She had been with the group for almost two years and liked it very much because she lacked nothing. She continued:

> There have been plenty of opportunities, as you can imagine, to make much money with love. I could have easily entered into the seraglio of a Nabob but I'm too proud to sell myself as a whore for money or to be treated as a slave. The politeness and kindness you showed us and your gentleness and goodness toward the audience, your knowledge of our language and customs, attracted me and opened my heart to you.

Fig. 21 From *Reize in eenen Palanquin*, vol. 2 (Amsterdam 1808). Jacob Haafner and Mamia, his Indian girlfriend, are reunited at the tank of the temple of Nawabpet.

Then she told him that she had heard that a European was killed by a poisonous snake, and from the description they gave it was clear to her that it must be Haafner. She had burst into tears and had been able to think of nothing else but him. That's why she had been so shocked when she saw him rush towards her in person. Haafner thanked her for the explanation and gave a detailed account of his poisoning. She noticed the swollen finger that was four times the normal size and black as coal. She promised to be back in a few hours because she wanted to consult a renowned doctor in a nearby village. But Haafner didn't want to tire her, and he would depart soon. Mamia then asked whether she could prepare a salve, a recipe she learned from her father. That Haafner could not refuse, and shortly after that she came back with the ointment. She herself applied it on the stinking wound. Their love was now sealed and they agreed to see each other again in Madras. Haafner continued his way through Paliacol, which had been the headquarters of the VOC on the Coromandel Coast since 1784. He visited a Dutch doctor who wanted to amputate his hand because he believed that gangrene had already spread through it. Haafner thought that the doctor was crazy and prepared for his departure for Madras, where he arrived the next day.

Lily of the South

He immediately went to see Beisser who reassured him and suspected that Mamia's ointment stopped the gangrene from spreading further. Haafner could stay with his cousin. After a few days Beisser removed the upper pastern bone of his middle finger. Two weeks later Haafner was declared healed. He could not have been happier, as Mamia arrived in Madras around that time. She was glad that Haafner had recovered so well. He rented a house for her, hired a servant, and gave money for the household:

> And thus I came into possession of this young dancer with the most noble of feelings and most virtuous behavior. Of this she gave me proof that took away all my doubts. Also her alluring and enchanting manners that were expressed in her posture, gait, and gestures. She understood the art of pleasing, flattering, and loving and of expressing herself pleasantly and aptly. In one word, she combined all the graces in her that these girls possess, which they practice from childhood. Never have I regretted it and I often blessed the moment I got to know her in Perla-Chirala and met her again at the pond near Nawabpet.

Although Haafner lived with Beisser whom he assisted in the morning when he went to visit his patients, he was mainly at Mamia's. In the afternoon he would go with her to a beautiful garden surrounded by a wall outside the city.

> This was a wonderful outing for me and Mamia. Many afternoons
> I spent with her in this garden.

He found the most attractive aspect of the garden to be a pond that was
surrounded by towering coconut palms. The wide and rustling tops were
reflected in the clear water.

> It is in this pond too that we bathe in the early morning. The
> two of us alone could romp and play in the refreshing water to
> our heart's content.
> At night we enjoyed the chess game that she could play
> very well. She also often sang a love-poem or epic while she
> accompanied her voice with a kind of a guitar. Sometimes she
> told some history or gave me riddles and so forth. She did her
> best to cheer me up with all resources at her disposal and to let
> the time with her pass pleasantly. Meanwhile, she did not forget
> the supper, which she made ready while talking and singing.

They talked about how they later were going to live in Ventapalemu, to which
Haafner ascribes the same qualities he had sung of in Sadras. First Haafner
had to make a trip that would take a month to finish unspecified matters.

The trip went through familiar territory for Haafner and would carry him
via Sadras to Pondicherry. He ordered his *dobash* (agent) to translate letters he
would write to Mamia and to write her answer to him. When he arrived on
the beach early in the morning, Mamia was waiting for him. She wanted to
accompany him into the dinghy to the boat, but Haafner didn't want her to
because the sea was too choppy and because the boat had been overloaded by
an English officer. But she could not be stopped. Besides the skipper and six
rowers on board were the officer, an old *mestizo* woman, Mamia and Haafner.
At the very first surf the sloop filled up with water and Haafner jumped
overboard with Mamia. The boat sank and they swam back to the beach. In
the sight of the harbor, things went wrong.

> I suddenly felt something heavy hanging on me. I looked around.
> Heaven! How great was my terror. It was the old *mestizo* woman
> holding on to my coat with both her hands. She let herself be
> dragged by me or rather she hung on me without the least effort
> to get ahead herself. I tried with my feet to liberate myself from
> her but to no avail.

What followed was a struggle to get rid of her with the help of Mamia. Haafner
lost consciousness and only came to again on the beach and was brought to

Beisser who gave him medicines. He immediately asked his *dobash* how Mamia was doing. She had saved his life but had been injured herself. Haafner now decided to travel overland, but Mamia had a bad premonition.

> Calm yourself, dear Mamia, I said. I love you very much. I am very much obliged to you and will never let you down. Believe me that within a month I'll be back with you again.
>
> You will not see me again! She cried in a heartbreaking tone. The light of my life will have been extinguished before you come back. It is the last time that I see you. I paid no heed to her words and considered them as an expression of her grief on my departure.

Thus Haafner left and during the trip called once again on the temples of Mahabalipuram which he had visited regularly during his time in Sadras. He gives a detailed description, which was the first accurate description of them in Western literature. He was particularly impressed by the architecture and the sculptural elements:

> At these temples more than life-sized animals such as elephants and lions are standing which are carved out of the mountain. Most of these ruins and especially the temples are carved from the rock. They are therefore formed as one piece, but there are also those which are made up of square blocks of bluestone. These stones are smooth inside, and without lime or cement they rest on each other because of their weight.
>
> When one considers what a force would have been necessary to hoist such astonishingly large blocks up 80 to 110 feet, one cannot help but be astonished. I do not know with what kind of equipment they have done so and I cannot comprehend it. These piles of rocks, if I may call them so, are evidence enough that the Indians of that time knew the principles of mechanical engineering. They had even more knowledge of it than they do at present, and we can say that they must have reached an advanced level of science.

Compared to this the European warehouses on the Coromandel Coast fell completely into insignificance.

Upon arrival at the hostel in Pondicherry where he had already arranged rooms from Madras, Haafner was handed a letter from Mamia. It showed that her health condition had worsened, and his *dobash* added that he had to come back as soon as possible. Haafner got a fever and had to stay in bed for ten days. Again he received a letter from Mamia, who had a severe cough now and begged him to return. Haafner first wanted to settle his affairs and wrote that it could take a few weeks before he came back, especially since he also had to go on to Cochin. The day before his departure his *dobash* reported that Mamia had been gone without a trace for three days and asked him to stay a few more days in Pondicherry to await messages. Haafner stayed, and two days later someone asked for him.

> Do you know the former dancer Mamia? My God, yes, I exclaimed, full of joy. Yes, I know her. Do you know where she is? She's at my house. At your place? I interrupted him impatiently. True? Come on! Take me to her immediately.

The good man told him she was at his mother's, some miles to the north of Pondicherry. She had arrived there yesterday with her nurse and was completely exhausted. She had asked him to look for Haafner.

When Haafner heard this, he immediately prepared everything for the trip. He arrived the next morning at seven o'clock. Her nurse met him and told him Mamia's condition was alarming after the grueling trip from Madras. It was a sad reunion.

> She lay on a mat. I was shocked to the bone when I saw her. Alas! This I could not have imagined. How she had changed! How radically changed was her beautiful and youthful face. Her brilliant fiery eyes were dull and lay deep in their sockets. This girl was a ghost of what she used to be. I could barely recognize her.
>
> She gave a cry of joy when she saw me and made an effort to sit straight up, but she could not. The nurse had to help her. She stretched her emaciated arms out to me, and I embraced her tenderly. She cried aloud at my neck. However much I had intended to keep myself strong, I could not prevent my tears from mingling with hers.

She told him she had contracted the ailment when she had rescued him, and the crossbeams of the barge had hit her under the breast. Haafner was very upset that she might die because she had saved him. Mamia's end was approaching fast and she told him her last wishes.

> "The first is," she said, "that you'll burn my corpse as is usual with us, but I urge you emphatically not to make any major expenses for it. Second,"—here she halted and looked at me with pleading eyes—"Well, what is it, dear Mamia?" "Ah," she

said, "I am afraid to ask you. That you will give me the last honor by lighting the wood pile for my corpse."

"Ah, yes, from the bottom of my heart, dear Mamia!" I exclaimed. "Who else but me should do this? Who else is duty bound to perform the last honors for you. I who owe you my life, you who saved me from the waves. I have so many obligations to you it would be an ungrateful if I would refuse this favor, at least if the bitter misfortune should overcome me that death would separate you from me."

My promise brought a ray of satisfaction and joy on her face. She wanted to thank me but her weakness prevented her from speaking.

It seemed as if death had waited until she had told me this because shortly thereafter I saw her change suddenly. Her eyes began to break and a shiver ran through her limbs. I sat next to her on the mat and she hurriedly grabbed my hand and squeezed it as she moved her lips spasmodically. "Farewell, my lord," she wanted to say, but she could not speak the words. Mamia was no more!

Haafner made good on his vow, and toward the evening he went back to the house where Mamia was laid out.

With tottering steps I went to the house where they were waiting for me. Mamia was brought outside. I picked her up and laid her limp and loose members, previously so quick and nimble, in my palanquin. My tears fell with big drops on her face.

The torches were lit and the corpse bearers carried her away. The loudly echoing mournful notes of the horns mingled with the lamenting of her nurse through the quiet village.

We arrived at the cremation ground. When the regular ceremonies were over, I picked her up with the help of one of the corpse bearers and placed her gently on the wood pile because I did not want them to treat her roughly as they are accustomed to do with corpses. When everything was ready, they handed me a burning corpse torch, and with my back turned to the pyre as is the custom, I lit it and gave my dear Mamia to the flames!

The ashes of her bones he had deposited in a round pot which he buried on a knoll among palm trees.

"As long as the palm trees on the hill quiver their rustling crowns in the wind, so long the villagers will remember the white man and his beloved Mamia," Haafner mused.

In the Land of the Dodo

On October 17, 1786 Haafner left via Pondicherry the Coromandel Coast which he would never, except in his thoughts, see again. He arrived on December 3 in Port Louis in Mauritius after a journey of 48 days, a journey which was plagued by storms and doldrums. Normally that journey took less than a month to complete. Mauritius, which has an area of 1,865 square kilometers, had in 1787 a population of 40,000, of which 20 per cent were white and the rest were slaves, mainly from Madagascar. From 1598 to 1710 it was in Dutch possession, after which the French took control of it and renamed it Isle de France. The colony was a naval base in the Indian Ocean of vital importance for France. The main products were sugar and spices, which were grown on large plantations spread across the island. The work there was mainly done by slaves from Madagascar. The period between 1783 and 1790 was extremely prosperous. Pirates were in no little measure responsible: they spent their extra income in the more than 125 pubs in Port Louis. Moreover, the governor was Count François de Souillac, a decadent French nobleman, awash with money. Cyclones, which would periodically destroy the infrastructure of the island, had left Mauritius alone for more than ten years. Seen from this point of view, Haafner could not have chosen a better time to sail into the history of Mauritius.

> A government official who had come on board, gave us documents, and assigned us a mooring site in the harbor beneath high rocks. They were like steep walls between which we were completely safe. Although it is difficult and dangerous to sail into the harbor, it is altogether good and safe once inside. The port and the entire colony are vital for the French. If they had not had Mauritius, they would have had to bow before the supremacy of their insidious competitors, the English, long ago and had to withdraw from India.

After this remark Haafner alludes to the discussion that prevailed in his time on the actual value of Mauritius for France. He is referring to Pierre Sonnerat's *Voyage aux Indes orientales et a la Chine*, which certainly did not see the island as an asset for France. Sonnerat rejects Mauritius and argues—

according to Haafner he was right about that—for a strengthening of the French presence on the coast of India itself: "The port, where we can make a warehouse for India, is the only advantage that can be taken from this establishment." Sonnerat continues: "Isle de France was and always will be fatal to any establishments that the French would have in India." We should not lose sight of the fact that Sonnerat's book was published in 1782, at a time when the French position on the Indian mainland was much stronger than when Haafner wrote about it.

Sonnerat supported the idea of transporting French troops straight to India instead of letting them acclimatize in Mauritius, which he thought was a blow to discipline. Haafner disagrees with Sonnerat. According to him, Mauritius was excellent as a warehouse for ammunition, food, water, and other necessities. He also thought that Mauritius was a good way station where troops could regain strength and get used to the tropical climate. Obviously, according to Haafner, Mauritius has the advantage of being much closer than France to India. Haafner arrives at a measured conclusion:

> I do not assign as much value to the possession of this island as
> it usually is awarded in books which are repeated again and again
> in turn. On the other hand, I do not slight the value as some do,
> including Sonnerat.

After this explanation, Haafner turns his attention to the landscape, the products, and the climate of Mauritius:

> Isle de France shows from the sea at first glance nothing but an
> accumulation of dry barren rocks and steep cliffs, but inland
> there are beautiful plantations, gardens, rustling rivers, and
> splashing waterfalls. Everywhere there are hares, partridges,
> guinea fowl, and other animals. There are ebony, *takamaka*,
> cinnamon, oak, and many other types of wood of excellent
> quality and in great abundance. The coffee, cotton, spice, and
> sugar plantations that have been done before and after my
> presence (and that succeeded pretty well despite the volcanic
> soil) are among her greatest resources. All this added to the
> healthy, pure and moderate climate would make this island one
> of the most pleasant and prosperous for residence, if these
> benefits were not almost completely offset by two plagues which
> ravage the island regularly, namely hurricanes and rats.

Haafner focuses his attention on Port Louis, the capital of Mauritius and its inhabitants.

> Port Louis has few interesting sights except a fine church and a well-equipped hospital.

The remark about the hospital must be seen in light of Haafner's merciless criticism of the healthcare of VOC. Nor is Haafner impressed by the fortifications of the city in spite of all the activities of the engineer Joseph-François Charpentier de Cossigny, highly reputed in his time Haafner gives a concise summary:

> Any enemy who sets foot on shore may be master of the city.

The coral reef that surrounds the island, according to him, is the main defensive asset of the island because it is an almost insurmountable barrier for ships that wish to land. The Champ de Mars, a parade ground for soldiers, also did not escape Haafner's interest because in the evening it changed into a Champ de Venus for

> . . . all the women of the city that could still pride themselves on their youth and good looks. The air was filled with a boisterous merriment that was contagious to foreign visitors.

But that was not all Haafner had to say about the female inhabitants of Port Louis:

> As moderate and temperate as is the climate, so depraved is the morality, at least when I was there. There is no girl or woman, whatever her position in society may be, who was above suspicion. However, they may be proud of their extraordinary beauty, which is common for women of European descent. The black women are even less modest than the other women. They spend all their money on their appearance and in particular dedicate large amounts of money on cotton from Paleacatte [now Pulicat, in India] with which they adorn their heads in a graceful manner.

The only exception to that dubious morality was the wife of his friend, the merchant Cockrell, with whom Haafner was staying. Haafner fails to go into the moral behavior of the male population on the island, which was certainly on par with that of the females. This notion of extravagance and corruption found its way into contemporary guidebooks on Mauritius.

One of the most fascinating remarks made by Haafner is the following:

> The houses [in Port Louis] are almost all made of wood and have only one floor because of the hurricanes. They are placed

on heavy rollers through which one can make them change places using ropes.

The only other reference to this type of house is in a book about the architecture of Mauritius. Houses on stilts are not uncommon, but mobile homes on rollers are undoubtedly rare. It immediately caught my attention, and I began to wonder why the people of Mauritius would regularly want to move their homes. It would certainly have contributed to the gay and vibrant atmosphere that already prevailed in the city, but it is clear that it must have had a practical motive. What was the purpose of houses on rollers? And why did the Mauritian government proclaim a ban on the construction of wooden houses precisely at this time?

To date the explanation a carpenter gave me is the most satisfactory. After I told him a little about the climatic conditions in Mauritius, he came up with the following explanation: "The mobility of the houses would make it possible to rotate them to face the wind during a cyclone. The wind blowing through the house would cause a negative pressure to press the house down to the ground, but not to such an extent that it would be blown to pieces. Even with gusts of over 200 miles per hour such a building could survive." If the statement is correct, one might wonder why Port Louis was not transformed into a city on rollers, because buildings made of stone collapsed or were severely damaged. Perhaps future archival research will provide an explanation for this intriguing architectural phenomenon. The same applies to the exact date when the devastating cyclone, which Haafner describes so vividly, struck the island. In the nineteenth century accurate records were kept of when cyclones struck the island. Such sources are lacking for the period before.

Heaven and Earth Perished

The cyclone that Haafner describes can be traced in the literature on Mauritius. Except opinions on the time and the year in which it occurred diverge between 1786 to 1789. H.C.M. Austen in his *Sea Fights and Corsairs of the Indian Ocean: Being the Naval History of Mauritius from 1715 to 1810* speaks of a cyclone at the end of 1786. Since the cyclone season lasts from November until April, the cyclone which Austen mentions must have taken place at the beginning or at the end of 1786. In the latter case, it would be close to the date that Haafner gives, namely January 14, 1787. Since the passage on Haafner's stay in Mauritius was published by his son on the basis of notes written by his father, and because Haafner rarely gets his dates wrong, I will assume that the date Haafner gives is correct until the contrary is proven. This is further substantiated by VOC sources referring to the ship *De Paerl*, which was hit by the same cyclone soon after. Further research should make it possible to trace the exact date, because if what Haafner says is true, the cyclone must have had great influence on the social and economic life of the colony. This should be traceable in other sources, such as cemeteries and ship logs.

Haafner first describes the signs that he had noticed a few days before the cyclone hit the island.

> The sun seems to rise larger than usual from below the horizon. Matte and dull its flame coloured disc stands, as though covered by a thin haze, in the opaque but cloudless sky. A hollow roar, like the rolling of distant thunder, rises from the deepest bowels of the mountains while its crowns are hung with a thick fog. The heat from the atmosphere becomes increasingly oppressive [the humidity in Mauritius is almost always around 90 per cent]; malaise spreads through the body and takes away my interest to do anything. Finally, at the approach of the fateful day, the signs become all the more threatening. The sky is continuously covered. The entire expanse swirls and ever faster the fleeting clouds follow upon each other while it is calm on the ground. Occasionally there are violent squalls interspersed with brief dust rains or sudden periods of silence. The haze around the tops of the mountains compacts into a row of copper-coloured clouds, which roll slowly up toward the mountains. The sea is boiling and bubbling much stronger than normal and casts strange shells and plants out of her innermost abyss onto the beach. From all directions rush anxiously screeching seabirds, who seek a safe refuge in burrows.

Haafner, who had witnessed the devastating hurricane that struck Madras in 1782, began to take precautions. He had his goods unloaded, but everybody laughed at him for what they saw as his crazy and cowardly behavior. The captains and inhabitants of the island should have known better, Haafner explains, but he behaved that way because it was so long since a massive cyclone had struck the island. They had become careless and therefore ignored all signs which they knew so well, but which had for a long time not resulted in a major catastrophe. The prevailing prosperity must also have contributed to this lax attitude. Based on this information, it seems likely that it had been at least ten years since a major cyclone had hit the island. Out of courtesy his host Cockrell followed Haafner's example, a courtesy that would pay itself back a thousand fold, as becomes apparent below. After the description of the warning signs, Haafner continues with a picture of the havoc wreaked by the nameless cyclone:

> Finally on the evening of the fourteenth the cyclone suddenly erupted, after a deadly and grim silence of several hours, with gross violence and roaring. It cannot be put into words because it is beyond compare. Heaven and earth perished. The wailing and howling of the storm, between which only occasionally the incessant rattle of thunder and the collapse of nearby houses was heard, would have filled the heart of the bravest with terror. The totally variable wind seemed, after a short interval of abatement, to collect new rage and power from each direction. Even in the house in which I found myself, which was built solidly and from stone, there was the constant danger that I was buried under its rubble. It creaked and moved so much that the beams shot from the seams and the attic split apart.
>
> This house where I was visiting belonged to Mr. Faber, and I saw myself forced to stay until the storm had passed. At first I tried to go back to the house of Cockrell, but I hardly had moved a few steps from Faber's house when the wind grabbed me with an irresistible force and threw me to the ground. It is certain that if I had not been able to grab the threshold of a house and hold onto it, I would have been blown into the river like a leaf. When the violence of the gust of wind seemed somewhat appeased, I quickly crawled on all fours to the house of Mr. Faber. Accompanied by a shower of tiles, branches, windows, and shelves and blinded by the incessant sparkle of rays of lightning that pierced the sky and completely bewildered by this wild uproar of the elements, I managed to slip into the house. Only those who are familiar with the indescribable force of the wind on this and some islands in the Caribbean, will believe that when I was back in the house, I saw a coattail that was literally blown off as if cut by a knife.
>
> By morning the storm began to abate somewhat, and when daylight came, a heartbreaking scene unrolled that would not leave even the most insensitive among us indifferent. All thirty richly laden vessels that had been anchored in the harbor the previous day were completely beaten to pieces. They were either thrown against the rocks, sunk, or had collided against each other. I saw a number of wrecks entangled on the beach.

Between the towers, masts, rudders, ropes, sacks, and barrels, which criss-crossed together in layers, I spotted here and there shattered limbs of people which completed the gloom of this gruesome scene. Gigs, ships' rigging, and other objects were carried into the center of the city by the unbounded agitated sea and ferocious wind.

The cyclone had left a trail of devastation on land. Entire plantations were destroyed. Trees were ripped roots and all from the earth and lay criss-crossed together like a row of cornstalks through which a group of hunters had passed who had been chasing a deer. To my knowledge not a tree had been left standing upright around the city, and because of the heat and sharp winds all the plants and low shrubs that were left standing were scorched as if by fire.

Apart from the poor sailors who were on board the ships, of whom none had been saved, this convulsion of nature also took the life of many residents of the island. Some were buried under the rubble of their own homes, others blown into the river, and again others crushed against the rocks. In a word, it was an extremely sad spectacle, the charming city which yesterday had lain so pretty, now reduced to rubble and her people, until recently so happy and cheerful, plunged into deep mourning and poverty.

According to Haafner the cyclone had a negative impact on the economy and social life of Mauritius.

All trading was temporarily suspended and all provisions were exorbitantly expensive and extremely sparse. A happy circumstance for the poor people was that the ships from Bengal were about to arrive with their loads of rice.

Haafner had brought his merchandise to safety and sold part of it, yet he could not sell the rest because the price of his goods had collapsed. No one wanted to buy them. What to do?

After this event I had little appetite for staying any longer on the island. Everyone looked depressed or had experienced heavy loss, and complained about the high cost of food or the fact that all trade and traffic were discontinued. The joy and pleasure had for now left the island. The cost of living had doubled and

there was little prospect that the situation would soon improve.
So I wanted to leave Isle de France, but where to?

This existential question resolved itself with the arrival of the ship *Deux Frères* from India, which had France as destination. Haafner negotiated a favorable agreement with the captain of the ship on the transport of his goods, which would yield much more in Europe than in Mauritius. On February 9, 1787, Haafner departed from Mauritius. He made a brief stopover in La Réunion and arrived in early March in his former home of Cape Town.

He could no longer recognize the Cape Town of his youth. He observed the same degradation as in Mauritius.

> The previously so demure girls and women were no longer recognizable. They had gained in imprudence what they had lost in modesty and quiet domestic virtues. Also the opulence and splendor that I saw spread in the buildings, furniture, and clothes, often gave me the impression of being in a completely different city than the one I left sixteen years ago.

He tried again to recover his money from Jakob Pieter De Neijs, who had fled to South Africa. It was in vain. He wanted to get away from Cape Town as quickly as possible. He did not have to wait long, for the *Deux Frères* left for Europe by the end of March with a colorful group of passengers.

Chapter 5

Languishing in Europe

Haafner arrived on May 25, 1786 at the Île de Groix, where all French ships coming from the East moored. He went ashore in Lorient. He sold the rest of his goods and drew demand bills against the bank Rey and Co in Paris. He then traveled to Germany where he was reunited with his brother. Matthias had become pastor in the East Frisian town of Esens after completing his theological studies in Halle, and later moved to the Frisian island of Norderney, where he had married the daughter of the governor of the island. Jacob had mixed feelings during the visit when Matthias told him that his mother had died the year before. After that Jacob made a visit to his sister Christina, who lived in Magdeburg. Here he stayed longer, because the town had a more varied social life than on Norderney. Then he went to a German spa for health reasons, which made him recall childhood memories in Emden. He went back to Amsterdam via Friesland.

At the time of Haafner's return, the Netherlands was in a political turmoil. Major political changes were occurring, yet in many respects, as will be seen later on, business was carrying on as usual. The 1780s are known as the Patriotic period, when the emerging bourgeoisie sought more influence, but was thwarted in this by the old establishment of the regents of the Dutch republic. Political reforms were blocked and a more democratic constitution was, for the time being, not realized. Political controversies ran so high in the 1780s that a civil war seemed imminent. The crisis reached a climax precisely in 1786, the year Haafner returned to the Netherlands. In that year, Prussian troops invaded the country and the Patriot revolt was halted. Many Patriots fled to France and would have to wait until 1795 before they could return to their home country.

Meanwhile, Haafner almost lost his life in the small Frisian village of Makkum where the effects of the disputes between the Patriots and the

Orangists who opposed them were palpable. Haafner experienced firsthand what the Orange masses were capable of.

Kees, Kees! Shouted the Orange Rabble

Before I left Makkum, a nice Frisian town, I almost found a sad end to my life. It was already winter and because I saw many people enjoying themselves ice skating on a canal not far from my hostel, I suddenly was seized with the desire of also doing this.

It was then in the Netherlands a time when not wearing a big orange plume was considered a great crime. I had therefore decorated my travel cap with a cockade of the largest type. Unfortunately I forgot to pin it on my hat, which I wore for skating. Scarcely was I on the ice, I had only driven up and down a few times, when all eyes focused on me. It surprised me, and I was groping in the dark as to what reason there might be for this. I heard the familiar *Kees!* [then a commonly used curse] resound, but I did not realize that it referred to me. It was not long before I was being pursued by several people. They blocked me in and soon I was surrounded by a large crowd. Only now, too late, did I understood that this was caused by the absence of my cockade. I took as much as feasible a calm and tolerant attitude. When a crude peasant asked with swearing where my cockade was, I took off my hat and acted as if I was amazed that it was not there. I replied that I probably had lost the cockade, and that if he just came along to my lodgings I'd show him my cap with the orange plume.

I thought I have delivered myself in this way from this predicament, but that turned out to be a miserable miscalculation. The crowd consisted of the crudest Friesian rabble, skippers, farmers, and such kind, that is, eager to commit violence when they think they have a reason to do it with impunity. Increasingly the *Kees, Kees!* swelled and at the same time it was said that I must be severely punished. In vain I asked someone to give me their orange ribbon so I could put it on my hat in their presence. I also gave a few boys money to go buy a ribbon for me. However, they did not come back, and eventually a soldier proposed to dip me a few times in an ice hole as punishment for my audacity for having ventured among them without an orange ribbon.

The scary proposal was welcomed by the whole gang, and despite my protest, the raging mob started to drag me, shouting and praying, to an ice hole while cheering—when to my luck two distinguished citizens managed to work their way through the mob with a great amount of pushing and shoving and wrested me from the clutches of this rabble. They decided to go with me to the inn to determine whether I was telling the truth. Accompanied by the whole crowd I arrived there. When I showed them my cap bearing the disputed orange ribbon, they began waving their hats frantically and raised a deafening clamour of "Orange Hurrah!" Thereupon the horde departed.

I went straight to the mayor to lodge a complaint, but instead of giving me satisfaction and punishing the leader of the savage executioners, the bumpkin replied blandly that I had escaped all too easily. He added that it was a good lesson for me.

I was beside myself with rage thinking about the danger that I had been in, after enduring so many dangers in distant countries to be put to death by this rabble in this small Friesian village.

When he arrived in Amsterdam, Haafner was 33 years old and fairly well off because of the trading that he had undertaken in Calcutta. He did not report in detail how he had gathered his fortune, but he went about explaining how most Europeans abroad garnered their capital:

Making a fortune! These two words will be the demise of the VOC and of all such businesses in the East. These have caused the devastation and depopulation of whole countries and kingdoms. Nobody goes to the East except to make his fortune. That unhappy continent has become the workhouse of Europe; wrongdoers, spendthrifts, thugs, anyone who has been banned from his birthplace by his crimes or in a different way, bankrupts and other bad people. Everything rushes to the Indies as to one common prey. Everyone wants to make his fortune and in which way is this possible? Only by robbing the company that they work for or by oppressing, plundering, and murdering the poor inhabitants. Of the ten who come back rich from there certainly nine have obtained their booty that way.

JACOB HAAFNER.

Fig. 22 From *Lotgevallen en vroegere zeereizen* (Amsterdam 1820). Portrait of Jacob Haafner. Engraving by Phillippus Velijn after a drawing by Dalin, around 1806.

A Full Purse

He himself was convinced that he had won his fortune in a fair manner. Initially, he was happy to be back again in Amsterdam but that did not last long.

> The beloved Europe! I thought then. Now I think about it quite differently. I was not yet 12 years old when I left. O! How very different I found Europe at my return. How far it was from the idea that I had formed of it. No, in Europe and especially in the northern part they do not enjoy life. One could say they are pining away: in a word, one dies without having really lived.

Now he was back in Europe, there seemed only one way Jacob could again evoke the tropical feeling; but that didn't work either.

> Fortunate are those who can travel. I have travelled through Holland, Germany, France and other countries . . . at leisure, without rush, and with a full purse, but there was only misery in Europe.

We know that he indeed visited his brother in Germany several times as traces of this are found in the archives. Recently, a poem was discovered that Jacob Haafner had written in the "friends book" of his sister who lived in Magdeburg. This is Haafner's only known poem, dated October 11, 1788.

Of all those other trips all the traces have been erased, except for a visit to the town of Veletri, not far from Rome. There Haafner visited the former museum of Cardinal Stefano Borgia (1731–1804) who had a large collection containing many works with an Asian origin. Did Haafner undertake a search for images from India in European collections? Because a description of the visit was later included by his son in *Proeve van Indische Dichtkunde, volgens den Ramayon* (*A Sample of Indian Poetry on the Basis of the Ramayana*, 1823), which was based on the *Nachlass* of his father, Jacob Haafner must have also made notes while traveling through Europe. The collection of Borgia has been dispersed but some of it is still to be found in the collection of the Vatican Museums where a small shrine of Vishnu is preserved, though not the canvas described by Haafner.

> On an Indian painting in the Borgia museum in Veletri that represents the struggle between Rama and Ravana, one sees the famous city where Ravana, which was located at an elevation on the island of Lanka. The city is attacked by monkeys and bears. Ravana stands with his army of giants and other fighters in a

vast field in front of the city. On the left side Lakshmana, Rama's brother, drives in a car pulled by four white horses and shoots an arrow at the giant Indrajit who rushes towards him. At the bottom of the canvas Rama and Ravana can be seen in battle. Wholly brown in colour, Rama shoots an arrow at the giant king, cuts off his hands and the donkey's head that sticks out above the ten other heads. Only then crashes down the many-headed monster with twenty arms, armed with arrows, axes, swords and shields. The monkeys attack the army of Ravana, the giants, people, elephants and horses with conventional weapons consisting of red bricks and palm branches. They hurl stones, kill and scatter the army and the battlefield is covered with corpses. Hanuman appears in the foreground, brown-coloured while he worships Rama the victor with clasped and raised hands.

Haafner probably did most of his traveling in Europe in the period before 1790, because in that year he met the 20-year-old Anna Maria Kreunink in Amsterdam. They had a son, Christiaan Matthias, who was born in September 1791. Their second child, Jacob, was born a year later but died in 1794, less than two years old. In 1797 their third child was born and named Jacob Matthias. Haafner probably moved in bohemian artistic circles. It is likely he regularly visited the capital's coffee houses like the famous Paradijsvogel (Bird of Paradise) where people from all parts of the world converged. He mentions it in his *Travels in a Palanquin* as being the place where he met a certain officer named Cartain in 1796. He was surely acquainted with the well-known engraver Reinier Vinkeles, who converted his drawings into engravings, and with his publishers Adriaan Loosjes and Nicolaas Godfried van Kampen.

In this environment it is possible that Haafner came into contact with August Wilhelm Schlegel, who later became the theorist of early German Romanticism. He lived from 1791 to 1795 in Amsterdam as a tutor with the Hoops, a family of bankers. It was in Amsterdam that Schlegel developed an interest in the study of Indian languages and philosophy, which was to play a major role in Romanticism. Who other than Haafner would have been able to make him enthusiastic for that culture? As the professor of Sanskrit Jean Philippe Vogel declared in 1900, Haafner was one of the first Dutch with a "pure interest in the ideas of the Indians". That Schlegel was also no stranger to Haafner's publisher Van Kampen is shown by a translation of Schlegel's *Uber dramatische Kunst und Literatur* (*On Dramatic Art and Literature*)

(1808) that Van Kampen published in Dutch in 1810, shortly after the publication of the original.

The Haafner Case

By 1795 Haafner's capital, which he had invested in French promissory notes, had become virtually worthless, and he started looking for other sources of income. It was understandable that in view of his overseas experience, his attention would go to the Comité tot Zaken van de Oost-Indische Handel (Committee for the Affairs of the East India Trade), which was founded in 1796 as a successor to the bankrupt VOC. Haafner believed that on the basis of his patriotic attitude and extensive knowledge of Indian affairs he would qualify for a place in the Directorate of the East India Committee. On June 20, 1796 his application arrived at the Committee. He recommended himself as follows:

> Diligence and vigilance in the service, a perfect knowledge of the Dutch, French, English, High German, and Portuguese languages, bookkeeping, a reasonable style, and a swift pen are the skills with which the applicant hopes to execute with honor and utter satisfaction whichever post to which your committee would be so gracious to appoint him.

The daily management of the Committee put Haafner on the list of candidates but he was passed over for appointments. In a letter dated September 19, 1796, he expressed deep disappointment over the decision because he did not doubt for a moment that he would get a post. He also stated that he had failed to get a job with the Amsterdam city council. He continued his application at the directorate, but after he found out that he would not be appointed, he volunteered for a post on the Coromandel Coast:

> The honorable committee may be pleased to allow him to accept the toughness of these conditions, and compare himself with an old warrior who as a reward of his services is sent again into the field, in order to be presented with new dangers and difficulties.

He requested an extract of the decision of the Committee. That request was rejected. He threatened to turn to the National Convention. Whether he carried out his intention is not known. It was not until July 20, 1797 that he approached the Committee again. He wrote that so far he had received nothing but ingratitude. He didn't ask for a job anymore, because as always:

> Fortune seekers, adventurers, bankrupts, and misfits (. . .) will
> be sent like hungry tigers among the hapless Indians.

The Committee would have to see how they would compensate him! When the trading posts would be returned, they would be sorry that they had treated such a good and competent officer with such indifference! He further said that he would continue his study of the character, manners, and customs of the Indian nations and would soon publish a paper on agriculture in India. That Haafner now really was in need of money is shown by the second part of his letter in which he asks for the return of the 1,000 pagodas which he had lent to Jakob Pieter De Neijs in Sadras.

On July 21 the request was read by the Executive Committee and handed to an official for advice. Until the end of August the work of the Committee would be almost exclusively devoted to the Haafner case. The official who reported his findings in the meeting on July 25 concluded that Haafner's claim was not supported by written evidence. The papers from Sadras and Nagapatnam, which could have given a definitive answer, had fallen into the hands of the English. The meeting decided to hear the supplicant himself. Thus Haafner appeared before the committee on July 26. The president, citizen Frederik Willem Fennekol, first inquired into the circumstances of the case and requested Haafner to support the legitimacy of his claim with valid evidence. On July 28 Haafner submitted his papers to the meeting. These consisted of copies of letters written by De Neijs, Johan Daniel Simons, and George Mackay. On August 14, 1797, the Committee rejected his claim because "It suffered of too great defect of liquidity to undertake its satisfaction, to be regarded as duty bound and just."

Haafner probably received a copy of the decision on the same day. He was insulted and felt that his reputation was compromised. After all, he would never claim something that he had already received. Moreover, he saw no reason in the decision of the Committee to refer the case to Batavia, because that detour would take many years.

> A sad and desperate prospect for the undersigned who with
> his family is desperately looking forward to the refund the
> outstanding debt with which he would be able to continue his
> business and trade with flattering prospects, which he otherwise
> fears to have to abandon.

The business was a trade in pipes, because he signed his letter with "pipe seller at the Camperhoofd". He again threatened to disclose the matter to the nation.

Such a debt deserves double the attention, as the well-being and preservation of the creditor depends on the payment of this.

This new request arrived at the Committee on August 28 and had already been rejected three days later because no new evidence was adduced. Haafner could turn to whomever he wanted. Whether he took further action is not known.

In 1800 the Raad der Aziatische Bezittingen en Etablissementen (Council of the Asiatic Possessions and Establishments) was founded. Haafner undoubtedly wished to leave Europe, and he turned with great expectation to the Council and repeated the requests that he had made to the Committee. "Your appointment, Respected Council, has raised my hope." It was a vain hope, and the request shows a certain naivety. The composition of the board of the Council was virtually identical to that of the Committee. Haafner meanwhile had achieved a first small success as a writer: in 1801 he published his first article in the leading journal *Algemeene Vaderlandsche Letteroefeningen*. He referred to this article in his letter to the Council, and Haafner also praised his extensive knowledge of commerce, language, and culture of Asians.

In the meantime he had to close his shop on the Camperhoofd, and he gave as his new address Korte Prinsengracht. He was now less demanding of his future job:

> To endow him with some minor post or to employ him as administrator of one of the Company's warehouses or stores, or as a translator in one of the main European Languages or otherwise.

If necessary, he would settle for a post on the Cape. The Council sent his request forward to Governor Jacob Abraham de Mist on the Cape on May 24, 1802. On October 28, Haafner had again moved and now lived in the Warmoesstraat; he repeated his request. He begged for a final decision because his application for a job had again been rejected by implication: "... because his unfavorable conditions threaten him and his family with penury." The Council adopted shortly afterwards its final decision, which was identical with the decision of the Committee on August 14, 1797. On November 26, 1805 his case was finally held to be expired. Haafner was in dire straits: earning a living as an author was not easy. However, his life would take a positive turn.

The article about Ceylon became a series, which was topical in the context of the peace negotiations. These would culminate in 1802 in the Peace of Amiens, in which the Cape was returned to the Batavian Republic but Ceylon became an English colony. That threw a spanner in the works for Haafner: he had hoped to return to Ceylon. The article series was abruptly discontinued after the peace treaty was signed. In the last episode, he makes mention of his intention to publish a weekly magazine about everything having to do with India. This magazine was never published.

The Dutch Society of Sciences

In the eighteenth century learned societies were established in many European countries, including in the Netherlands. In 1752, the Dutch Society of Sciences was founded with the aim of promoting the sciences. The board consisted of directors, who provided monetary donations, and members, who were mostly well-known scholars. The Society tried to achieve its objectives by initiating competitions, particularly in the fields of physics and mathematics. But matters regarding the colonies were also addressed, such as the question brought forward in 1794—and never answered—of how the health situation in Batavia could be improved. The winners received a gold medal or a substantial financial contribution and their writings were published in the Society's prestigious series *Verhandelingen* (Reports). Haafner must have gotten wind of the Society and seen it as a way to earn money. He didn't seem to be well informed about the functioning of the Society.

Haafner described himself as follows:

> During a 23-year stay in the Indies I have focused mainly on learning & studying the chief languages of the Indians, their religion, customs, morals, laws, ancient histories.

He offered the Society two rare Sanskrit manuscripts for sale. He did not doubt the Society would have an interest in these. Furthermore, he informed the board members that he was writing a book about the mythology of the Hindus; a dictionary of Sanskrit and Bengali words; and a book about the agriculture of India (following the *Georgics* of Vergil), which was almost finished.

He noted that his poor financial situation did not allow him to do it for free which had previously been the case. He hoped that the Society would encourage him because otherwise he saw few opportunities in the Netherlands.

> As I live in obscurity, never involved myself with writing except for my own pleasure, in addition to the critical times, and living in a country where seldom any merit is respected except commerce, my prospects seem not very gratifying.

Fig. 23 From *Reize in eenen Palanquin*, vol. 1 (Amsterdam 1808). A fortune-teller near Sadraspatnam, around 1780.

From this emerges Haafner's self image of someone who lives on the margins of society. It is also clear from this quote Haafner would never have become a writer if circumstances had not forced him to do so.

Two months went by between his writing and the meeting of the Society. The secretary Martin van Marum, then a prominent scholar, wrote him shortly after the meeting of the Society on October 4, 1796 that for the sale of the manuscripts he would have to approach a bookstore, and for the publication of his book, a publisher. In a letter dated October 16, 1796 Haafner detailed reasons as to why he felt it unfair that the Society has rejected his publication. Moreover, he could not understand why the "famous" Society would not be interested in the fruits of his labor:

> I thought, that like those of Calcutta in India, and of other nations in Europe, the Society not only aimed to promote science and scholarship but also would encourage a person who through experience, study, or distant and exceptional travels had made some useful discoveries, could make public unknown descriptions and writings, through which the veil of ignorance would be removed.

He pointed out to the Society that the knowledge of India, that enlightened nation where the sciences were highly developed, was as yet very slight in Europe. And how could booksellers judge his work?

> Their despicable behavior toward authors is well known.

After all, they only publish books by famous authors or persons supported by learned societies!

Van Marum informed the board of Haafner's reaction and was directed to go and talk with Haafner, but this took another six months. Haafner didn't give up and tried to sell his work elsewhere. He had a bit of success as a part of his *Hindu Mythology*, now called a translation of the *Ramayana* epic, was read in public.

> The Amsterdam Poetry- and Literary Society has held on the 9 May 1797 its Annual Assembly, here at the Handboog-Doelen. The President G. Brender a Brandis opened the meeting, reading some examples from the *Mahabarata* and *Ramayana*, two Sanskrit epics, translated by Jacob Haafner, arguing also that the Dutch Nation is now better placed to publish Indian poetry, translated directly from the Sanskrit, than the English.

Strengthened by this public reading he offered the same month another unfinished manuscript to the Society. He apologized for this in advance.

Incidentally, I request Your Lordship to excuse my inadequate style and writing because of the manifold activities with which I am inundated.

The manuscript, which was extensively annotated, dealt with the thousand names of the god Shiva. He later included a summary in his *Travels in a Palanquin*:

> To him are given a total of one thousand names that indicate his characteristics and abilities. Therefore, he is also named Doshotamé and Hazarramé or the Thousand-Named One. To satisfy the curiosity of my readers I will cite a few of those names as they come to my mind. Suituntrum, the independent; Surbepbirsi, the all present; Servasher, the lord of the universe; Ekkumesha, the only one; Nitteh, the eternal.

Both in the manuscript and in the *Travels in a Palanquin* dozens of other names follow. It must have disoriented the lordships. Van Marum sees it as an example of his skill in Indian scholarship. He informs Haafner, who had again asked for financial encouragement, that such support is only possible as the result of winning a competition, and that only those who had made themselves useful to the Society had eligibility. Furthermore, Van Marum adds that a chunk of translation as Haafner had given could never qualify for an incentive prize. It had to be a coherent whole.

Yet Van Marum's curiosity in this India expert was aroused because four months later, on October 30, 1797, he visited Haafner together with the President of the Society Jan Berkhout at the Camperhoofd. Van Marum reports on the results of their visit to Haafner the following day during the meeting

> ... that this man has had the opportunity (based on what he told us) to acquaint himself with the Sanskrit language, the sacred language of the Hindus, through his contact with a Brahmin, and that he gave to present us with clear information on the mythologies of the Hindus.

Haafner must have interpreted the visit as a positive signal because in late November 1797 he offered another text to the Society with the title "Feeling of the Hindus on Punishments in the Afterlife".

Van Marum convened a committee which had to assess Haafner's manuscripts because in addition to those already mentioned, Haafner sent a treatise on *devadasis*, Indian dancers, although van Marum had advised against it because of its controversial content. Haafner asked him if he needed to send a drawing of a dancer but was advised there was no interest in it. His entry was discussed at the meeting of February 13, 1798, but the evaluators felt the text was not credible and unscientific. Earlier, on January 18, Haafner had impatiently approached the Society to ask whether his text had been assessed yet. Van Marum informed him that, to his regret, the committee found them unsuitable to be published in the Proceedings of the Society. After this Haafner gave up, but his attempts probably contributed to his winning a prize a few years later from the Teylers Foundation, which was also based in Haarlem. After all, van Marum, who harbored some sympathy for Haafner, was also very influential there as the director of the Teylers Museum.

Laureate of the Teylers Theological Society

Haarlem apparently provided a fertile ground for private scientific initiatives. Less than four years after the Society's establishment in 1756, the Haarlem textile manufacturer Pieter Teyler van der Hulst decided to designate his legacy to the promotion of science and religion. The Teylers Foundation was established after his death in 1778. The management of the Foundation consisted mainly of Baptists, who were barred from other societies. It managed the artistic and scientific collections bequeathed by Teyler, which were housed in the Teylers Museum on the Spaarne River.

This museum opened its doors in 1784, and it can be admired in its original state to this day. It also housed two distinct societies. The first was the Teylers Theological Society, which through discussion and holding competitions wanted to promote the study of the Christian religion. According to the maxim which is written on the gold medal of honor of the Society— "Waare Godsdienst-kennis bloeyt door vrijheid" ["True knowledge about religion thrives through freedom"]—it wanted to emphasize that it was in favor of tolerance and against government interference in religious affairs. The second association, the so-called Second College, wanted to stimulate science, history, and literature.

At the end of 1803 the Theological Society launched the following competition:

> What results have missionaries had in the past two centuries in
> the spread of Christianity, and what results can we expect from
> the missionary societies working now?

The text of the call was printed in the main Dutch newspapers. Probably Haafner found out about it in a coffee house. It was a very topical subject.

Missionary thought was gaining ground in Europe at the end of the eighteenth century especially in Protestant circles. It was a movement that found its inspiration in Pietism, which had its center in Halle, Haafner's city of birth. In the Netherlands, the Evangelische Broedergemeente (Moravian Church) was established in 1787 in Zeist. Ten years later the Nederlandsch Zendeling Genootschap (Netherlands Missionary Society) was founded in Rotterdam in 1797. The missionaries boasted about the results they achieved with their work in the society's periodicals. These uplifting messages were intended for the home front, from which the missionaries received their funding. In reality, missionaries who were poorly trained and prepared achieved little or nothing.

Haafner had seen missionaries at work in South Africa and India and had become very critical of their ways and results. Because of his dire financial situation, and with his eyes on the prize—a gold medal or 400 guilders—he would not have hesitated long before putting on paper what he had wanted to do all along. He worked on it for about a year, and on November 30, 1804 Haafner's 195-page manuscript was delivered to the museum on the Spaarne. After a lengthy discussion the directors of the Teylers Theological Society decided at their meeting of April 4, 1805 to award Haafner the prize.

On April 9, 1805 the *Haarlemse Courant* announced that one Jacob Haafner had won the competition of the Society. Haafner had received a letter from the secretary of the board of the Society, Jacob van Westerkappel, Jr before publication:

> I have the pleasure to inform your honor that the directors and members of the theological society of the Teylers Foundation have met this afternoon to assess the received papers in the contest. The writer who had chosen the motto: *Il est difficile de servir un dieu qu'on connait pas*, etc., has, under the condition that he make changes and improvements, been awarded the gold medal. After the accessory bill was opened, it turned out that you are the author of the treatise. It is therefore my great pleasure to congratulate you on behalf of the society, and I assume that you can accept our terms and conditions. Next Tuesday the public will be informed of this in the *Haarlemsche Courant*.

A great burden must have fallen from Haafner's shoulders when he read this letter. On the one hand it meant recognition for his work, and it also brought him the sum of 400 guilders, which would have relieved his precarious financial situation. The requirements specified by the association he carried out without much grumbling. Already in his manuscript he had shown himself willing to improve or change the text. Given the explosive content, it was logical that the directors of the Teylers Foundation harbored reservations because Haafner's essay contains completely damning verdicts on the missions from beginning to end.

The reader is not left in the dark for long about Haafner's ideas. He starts his frontal attack on the missions and missionary societies even in the introduction:

> Of all religions and sects known to me there are none of which the followers have more zeal, or better more fanaticism, to propagate their religion than the Mohammedans and Christians. With merciless violence they have forced their beliefs on other people. The difference between Muslims and Christians is, however, that the first see the converted nations as their brothers after they have converted them and respect their property, and they do so to this day. With the Christians, however, this is far from being the case. With them there is hatred of religion rather than lust for religion which, added to their lust for power and thirst for gold, has brought devastation and disasters all around the world. Actually, it is such that they would prefer to erase from the earth those who disagree with them, rather than convince them through their argument. To their great misfortune the Indians of South America experienced this when the superstition and the "greed" came aboard in the fifteenth century when they covered the new world with 35 million corpses for the honor of God and persecuted the remainder of these once mighty nations deep into the forests.

In fanaticism Christians and Muslims could compete, but the Muslims were at least humane after they had achieved their goal. That could not be said about the Christians. Haafner paints a sharp picture.

> In one word: the disasters that Christians in their fanatical religious hatred have brought on not only the newly discovered countries but also all over Europe have been innumerable. Under the pretext of spreading the faith they committed the vilest crimes, and under the same guise all crimes were legalized. The highest level of villainy was called the epitome of virtue, and they made saints and martyrs of those who would be rewarded before a secular judge with painful punishment. The most horrible wickednesses were approved, even sanctified,

if only they were aimed at the interests of the church and promoted its growth and power. They thought to have sanction to murder anyone and to prosecute those who differed with them in religious terms or who resisted their spiritual tyranny.

The Directors must have had to swallow hard when they were presented with this prose, and it is understandable that they insisted on some changes and adjustments before they were prepared to publish it in their prestigious series *Verhandelingen* [*Discourses*]. Haafner cooperated, but it took two years and a lot of talking back and forth before his *Onderzoek naar het Nut der Zendelingen en Zendelings-genootschappen* [*Examination of the Usefulness of Missionaries and Missionary Societies*] was published in July 1807 as part XXII of the *Discourses of Teylers Theological Society* in an edition of 290 copies. In the foreword the directors distanced themselves from Haafner's *Examination*. They wrote that despite the improvements Haafner had made on their instructions in his original manuscript there were still quite a few bold statements and dubious advice remaining in it. It would prove to be the understatement of the year. They also disagreed with Haafner's statement that if the mission had not had any result in the past, it would also not be successful in the future. They saw the book as a useful work for future missionaries, who might learn from the mistakes of the past.

When the manuscript and the final printed copy are compared, the latter appears no less critical. On the contrary, some parts are even sharper because of Haafner's addition of quotes from a range of authors, as demanded by the Society. This makes Haafner's erudition evident.

The God of One's Tyrants

The French motto which Haafner gave to his *Examination*, "*Il est difficile de servir un Dieu qu'on ne connaît pas, plus difficile encore d'aimer le Dieu de ses Tirans*", was inspired by Voltaire, and covers the critical content of the text perfectly, the difficulty of loving the God of one's tyrants. In the introduction Haafner says that his book was based primarily on his own observations during his many years overseas as well as on his reading of other works. By this he meant Enlightenment philosophers such as Voltaire, Montesquieu, Jean-Jacques Rousseau, and anti-colonial writers such as François Le Vaillant, John Gabriel Stedman, Benjamin-Sigismond Frossard, Thomas Gage, Pierre Sonnerat, and Bartolomé de las Casas. The Enlightenment philosophers exercised a great influence on Haafner's thought. They were critical of Christian civilization, and held up the so-called uncivilized peoples or nations as a mirror to the

Europeans. In contrast to the Enlightenment philosophers, Haafner, like the other authors, based his writing on his own experience in the world overseas. Without exception these writers were critical of the behavior of the Europeans in the colonies, and they spoke up for the oppressed peoples. Bartolomé de las Casas (1474–1566) was the founder of this critical anti-colonial intellectual tradition. His *A Short Account of the Destruction of the Indies*, which was based on a 50-year stay in Central America, contains an emotional indictment of the crimes of the conquistadors. Haafner felt closely connected to de las Casas. At the end of the *Examination* he writes:

> I declare before God and the whole world, and with the Bishop de las Casas that what I have said of the Europeans in the colonies, is not a thousandth of what might be said.

Thomas Gage, author of the book *The English-American, His Travail by Sea and Land: or, A New Survey of the West-Indies*, was also a missionary in the Spanish colonies. In his book he is highly critical of the missionary work of the various religious orders. Haafner was also inspired by John Gabriel Stedman, who in his book *The Narrative of a Five Years Expedition against the Revolted Negroes of Surinam* gave detailed attention to the abuses the planters and other settlers inflicted on their slaves. The French Protestant theologian Benjamin-Sigismond Frossard turned in his book *La cause des esclaves nègres et des habitans de la Guinée* [*The Cause of the Black Slave and the Inhabitants of Guinea*] against the heartlessness of the Europeans towards the slaves. François Le Vaillant was also an inspiration for Haafner. Vaillant showed himself in his work *Voyage de M. Le Vaillant dans l'Intérieur de l'Afrique par Le Cap de Bonne Espérance, dans Les années 1783, 84 & 85* [*Travels into the Interior Parts of Africa, by Way of the Cape of Good Hope: in the Years 1783, 84 and 85*] to be an admirer of the Khoikhoi. He criticized in the harshest terms the inhuman behavior of the Boers toward them. Haafner fits in this list of European anti-colonial authors who wrote on the basis of their own experience.

Haafner saw the whole conversion effort only as a means to open up the overseas world for European ideas, and, even more, for their political and economic domination. He fiercely denounced the propaganda spread by the missionaries in their journals, which depicted the inhabitants of that world overseas as brutish monsters. The missionaries do so, according to him, primarily in order to get honest and God-fearing people to part with their money. But due to a lack of training and knowledge, the missionaries will never really succeed in making converts. Not entirely devoid of irony, Haafner argued that the missionaries could better stay in Europe because there was still plenty of work to do as far as conversion was concerned.

A special feature of Haafner's book is that it represents, for the first time, a global comparative study of Christian missions. He does not limit his work to one area, but describes the methods of the missionaries and the reactions of the people in such diverse areas as China, India, Tahiti, America, and South Africa. The first chapter describes the vain attempts to make the Khoikhoi accept the Gospel. Without a regular supply of tobacco and alcohol, nothing could be achieved here: as the motto went, *"Point de tabac, point de Hottentots"* ["no tobacco, no Hottentots"]. The reasons why the Khoikhoi spurn the Christian message was twofold. On the one hand this was the result of the lifestyle and language of the Khoikhoi; on the other, it was caused by the behavior of the missionaries themselves and the European-Christian population of the Cape.

The Khoikhoi are satisfied with what they have, Haafner said, and attached to their own way of life and traditions. They do not need a new religion. Furthermore, their language is so peculiar and difficult that no single missionary succeeds in learning it. It made the successful preaching of the Gospel very difficult. Then, Haafner argues, the missionaries themselves are incompetent and not up to their task. In addition, the Boers, Christians after all, who should have lead by example, were thoroughly corrupt. Haafner's argument keeps coming back to these two main points: first, that the people do not need Christianity and missionaries; and second, that other Europeans in the colonies are so thoroughly evil that they are themselves the biggest obstacle to the preaching of the Christian message.

The second chapter focuses on the mission among slaves on the plantations in present-day Suriname and the Caribbean. Haafner paints a negative picture of the plantation owners who unscrupulously exploit their slaves. The missionaries legitimize the regime of the planters and do nothing for the slaves. Haafner gives an even more poignant picture of the missions to the South Americans in the third chapter. Following de las Casas, he says the Indians were exterminated by greedy missionaries and soldiers with a sword in one hand and a crucifix in the other.

In the fourth chapter, Haafner states that the missions in India are doomed to fail because the Indians are very committed to their own traditions. Moreover, the Indian civilization is older than the European, and he considers Hinduism superior to Christianity. In the fifth chapter Haafner discusses the completely failed mission in Tahiti, and in the sixth he dwells on the Roman Catholic missions in China and Japan for which he has some appreciation. That is because the usually well-educated Jesuits included elements of Chinese and Japanese philosophy and religion in their teaching. Moreover, the Jesuits acquired through the study of language and culture of those countries the respect of the political elite, whereby they succeeded in recruiting converts. The Protestant missionaries, who tended to be orthodox fundamentalists, were usually not educated.

A Shot across the Bow of the Mission

Haafner's judgment on the usefulness of the mission was explicitly damning. Reactions quickly followed. His *Examination* was certainly not, as Teylers Theological Society had intended, regarded as a useful publication in missionary circles, full of advice for future Protestant missionaries. The *Examination* immediately became the subject of heated debate at the special meeting of the Dutch (Protestant) Missionary-Society which was held in Rotterdam from August 11–14, 1807, perhaps called together in view of the publication of the *Examination* in June. The key question was what the Society had to do to abate (or if possible completely eliminate) the very unfavorable impression of the missions which the *Examination* had created.

According to the well-known Dutch recipe, the directors of the Society decided to establish an advisory commission to investigate the adverse effects of Haafner's *Examination* for the missions and to refute his accusations. The report that was submitted at the end of the meeting has not been preserved. The directors did decide not to react publicly to Haafner's *Examination*. The meeting however was very pleased with the speech given by the Dordrecht minister Godefridus Johannes Schacht on August 13. This did not explicitly mention Haafner, but Schacht's speech, which was published the same year, was the first public reaction and rebuttal of Haafner's *Examination*. In it, Schacht emphasizes the social benefit of the missions; he regards them as a fulfillment of God's promise.

During the last session of the meeting on August 14, the professor of theology Johannes Anthony Lotze of the University of Franeker urged for a mission to Malabar and Coromandel. In a comprehensive consideration, he praises the social and geographic conditions in India, which would make a mission to these areas a promising enterprise. It should be noted that was precisely where Haafner had lived, an area which he had said that a mission wouldn't have any chances in. Lotze's argument can be seen as a second response to Haafner's *Examination*. Though Haafner had highlighted the unyielding commitment of the Indians to their traditional and deeply rooted religious mindsets, Lotze dismisses this argument by stating that Haafner himself had no adequate and true knowledge of the religious system of the people of India.

The Directors of the Dutch Missionary Society concluded that Haafner based himself too much on his own experience without consulting which they considered to be appropriate literature. So they decided that the argument against Haafner's *Examination* should focus primarily on his assertion that the missions to the targeted nations were totally useless because those nations clung to their traditional values. In the special meeting of 1808, attention was again focused on Haafner's *Examination*. Meinard Tydeman presented a list of articles and books drawn up by his brother Hendrik Willem Tydeman containing material that refuted Haafner's allegations—although there were also publications that seemed to confirm Haafner's opinion.

In 1809 no less than three publications were published that can be seen as attempts to refute Haafner's *Examination*. A. Blussé and Zoon, a publishing house in Dordrecht, published an anonymous discourse entitled *Verhandeling van het nut, hetwelk de reeds aangewende pogingen, ter voortplanting van het Ware Chistendom, onder de onbeschaafde volken te wege gebragt hebben* [*Treatise of the Usefulness which the Past Attempts at the Propagation of the True Christendom among the Uncivilized Nations have Produced*]. In the introduction, the author states that:

> The purpose of this is not at all to be a refutation, or a counter to the award-winning treatise of Mr. Haafner; a work, however easy, must be thus disagreeable to the writer, as would the reading of it be for the reader, and which is above all else a fruitless labor.

Despite his apparent reluctance to refute Haafner's *Examination*, the author could not resist pointing out Haafner's mistakes in an appendix of 14 pages. He notes that Haafner's argument was based on incorrect assumptions. Haafner namely started out from the character, mentality, and customs of indigenous peoples and then showed that attempts to convert them would be fruitless. Haafner's way of thinking, which was that of the other civilization, was unacceptable because it placed the non-European civilization on an equal footing with the Christian European one. The anonymous author considers this way of thinking as morally reprehensible and subversive, as the starting point of all proper thought was the Gospel, in which everything was clearly formulated:

> Why worry about morals and philosophies of pagan peoples who, after all, could come to the correct judgment only after they were illuminated by the light of the Gospel?

The author considers it a more than annoying shortcoming that Haafner does not share this vision:

> A lack that must leave us utmost surprised, how such a piece
> could carry away the honorable prize.

Then the author dwells on the limited historical knowledge that Haafner has about the mission and concludes:

> And such a man, who does not even know the history with
> respect of the missionaries of his own nation, and shows the
> greatest ignorance, would serve as counselor to the Missionary
> Societies!

The criticism of the author focuses also on the careless way Haafner handled the small amount of literature. As an example he cites David Crantz's book, *De Historie van Groenland* [*The History of Greenland*], which Haafner cites as sloppy. The anonymous writer shares a vicious sneer:

> Surely these are commanding words, if someone boasts on a
> 23-year stay in the Indies, to speak haughtily about Greenland.

A little further he accuses Haafner of bad faith because he was utterly hostile to the spread of Christianity, citing Haafner himself:

> The missionaries are satisfied if only they baptize and make
> Christians whatever kind of Christians they may be.

This might be true for the Catholic missions, according to the author, but not in the least for the Protestant Dutch missions because it is belied by history. He sighs:

> It's still a fruitless effort! Would this convince Mr Haafner?
> Would this convince all those who run away with this deficient
> work, and who think of it as the *non ultra plus*?

The latter intriguingly suggests that Haafner had supporters. If this was so, none of them were openly supporting Haafner.

Phallus Worship

Among the critics we also find the then famous sentimental writer and official Rheinvis Feith. In an attachment to his book *Verhandeling over de verbreiding der Evangelieleer over den aardbodem* [*Treatise on the Spread of the Gospel Teaching across the Earth*] he treats Haafner's *Examination*. His criticism was especially focused on Haafner's assertion that the missionaries were responsible for the unchristian acts of the colonial governments, and that the Hindus could not be converted because they were satisfied with their own faith. Feith gives as counter-argument the example of the Greeks who, with their impressive civilization, were finally converted by the apostles.

> This seems to me to be the major flaw of the otherwise in so many ways worthy *Examination* of Mr. Haafner.

Feith looked with a lot more sympathy to Haafner's work than the rabid anonymous author quoted above, because Feith also knew him as an outstanding author. He realized that the behavior of the Europeans in the colonies left room for improvement, but otherwise also for Feith it was a matter of fact that "God will complete His works".

At the end of his *Treatise*, Feith gives an extract of a letter he had received on the subject and which was probably written by the aforementioned Johannes Anthony Lotze. The letter writer admitted at the beginning that:

> The man's labor includes, in my view, a lot of truth, discovering many a mistake, and is suitable to inspire caution in the Directors of the Missionary Societies, both in the choice of missionaries as in devising of appropriate measures to meet the main goal of their work.

But that the missions are meaningless, as Haafner concluded, Lotze rejects wholeheartedly. Then he addresses Haafner's views about the religion of the Hindus. He sees Hinduism as a degeneration of the Christian religion and quotes Haafner himself, for whom the worship of the *lingam* (phallus) is also ridiculous:

> Good, innocent, gentle Indian women! Continue—to pray for the welfare of your husband's (to the Lingam)!—May He, who knows the inside of hearts, accept and hear your prayers to the Lingam, as though directed to Himself.

He then quotes Voltaire, who wrote with so much praise of the Vedas "at the expense of our Bible". Lotze rejects the idea that the book is an original Hindu work, in which the doctrine of the unity of the Supreme Being is proclaimed. Here emerges another difference of thought with Haafner. Lotze could not accept that the heathens could have discovered such a clear understanding except from Europe. After all, he says, "the sciences were brought to the Indies by the Greeks".

It is obvious to him that many concepts and terms in the system of the Hindus have been taken from the scriptures or the thinking of Christians. But the Christian tenets have been corrupted and supplanted by fables. Therefore it is high time to re-acquaint the Hindus with the original gospel. They would be only too happy to satisfy themselves with the "supreme wisdom of the Gospel which is the source of enlightenment and civility". Lotze shows himself an obvious supporter of the then prevailing "degeneration doctrine" which held that all the Indian scriptures that did not agree with the Christian scriptures must be corruptions of them. Conversely, Haafner argued that the question of the mission had to be approached from the perspective of a different way of thinking, from "the other". That could not be understood by Lotze and other convinced Christians. The French translator of Haafner's work was not very wrong when he called Haafner "an original and profound thinker"!

Fig. 24 Bob Pingen, Portrait of Jacob Haafner. Oil on canvas, 80 x 100 cm, 1995. Private collection.

On August 17, 1809, two weeks before Haafner died, the Gouda pastor Jacob Weldijk delivered a speech during the General Assembly of the Dutch Missionary Society in Rotterdam under the title "The Aid to Promulgators of the Gospel among the Heathen Nations that Could Rather be Seen as a Creed". According to Weldijk the missionaries don't go overseas to steal from the people, but to bring them into "the glorious freedom of God's children". According to him, Haafner's prediction that the nations will rise up under a great leader to free themselves from the colonial yoke can only come true if they accept the Gospel, which "leads the people to civilization". During an extraordinary meeting later that year a committee was appointed which was to evaluate the missionary activities. It finally concluded in 1815 that Haafner was right after all.

Farewell Lovable Objects!

On August 11, 1808, Haafner finally married Anna Maria Kreunink in Buiksloot, a village bordering Amsterdam which was at that time a popular place to get married. Although there was no will drafted, it made the succession clear. Haafner probably felt his end approaching. After all he suffered from angina pectoris, which entails pressure and pain on the chest. His inveterate smoking had undoubtedly aggravated his condition. Shortly after his marriage his masterpiece *Travels in a Palanquin* was published, which can be regarded as one of the best publications in the early romantic literature in the Netherlands. He dedicates the book to Louis Napoleon and calls upon him to protect the peoples in the colonies. The work received good reviews and was almost immediately translated into German.

In the last year of his life Haafner feverishly worked on his *Reize te voet door het eiland Ceilon* [*Travels on Foot Through the Island of Ceylon*] which he had intended to finish before the end of 1808. The largest part is occupied by his account of his adventurous hike through Ceylon undertaken in 1783. The book starts with a 60-page description of the natural history of the island. Haafner regularly excuses himself for the fact that he cannot be more detailed. Apparently he gave everything to complete the manuscript. The last lines of this description were probably the very last he ever wrote. "Farewell then, lovable objects that enthralled my soul!—Farewell!"

On September 4, 1809 he died at his home on the Hoogte Kadijk, next to the Overhaalsgang in the house named De Drie Bloeyende Koornaaren [The Three Flowering Wheat Ears]. He was buried on September 7 in the Nieuwe Kerk, but a tombstone has not been preserved. A year later, his son Christiaan published the book which Jacob Haafner concluded with the significant words that he looked forward to the time of his death with resignation and a joyful heart.

Postscript

In this biography I have omitted the footnotes. I have been able to do so because a very complete academic three-volume re-edition of his works, *Werken van Jacob Haafner*, offers those readers who want to dig deeper more than enough material. All of Haafner's books and the literature about him to which I refer in this biography can be found on a website specifically devoted to Haafner (www.paulvandervelde.nl). On this website all publications and news about Haafner are updated on a regular basis.

Sources

Amsterdam

Stadsarchief. Archief van de Lutherse Gemeente (213). Communicantenregister 608.
Burgerlijke Stand.
Universiteitsbibliotheek. Westerse handschriften, afdeling Nederland, 9 T, 1–3.

Colmar

Archives Municipales de Colmar. Burgerlijke stand.

Colombo

Sri Lanka National Archives.

The Hague

Nationaal Archief.
Archieven van de Verenigde Oost-Indische Compagnie, Overgekomen Brieven en
Papieren: 3342, 3375, 3400, 3542, 3607, 3718, 4246, 4253, 4258, 4263, 5221, 5226,
5230, 5257, 5259, 6478, 6491, 6554, 12571.
Comité tot Zaken van de Oost-Indische Handel en Bezittingen 1796–1800: 3, 44,
139a, 139b.
Raad der Aziatische Bezittingen en Etablissementen 1800–06: 31, 96, 98, 101.

Haarlem

Noord-Hollands Archief. Hollandsche Maatschappij der Wetenschappen, nrs. 15,
71–74, 444, 461, 475
Teylers Stichting Archief. Resoluties en Notulen 2, 3 en 6. Kopie van Haafners
manuscript, 1120. Bezoekregister Teylers Museum, 1803–09: 149.

Sources

Halle

Archiv St. Marien Kirche. Taufregister 1746–59.
Archiv Frankeschen Stiftungen. Missionarchiv I C 34c, 99a.
Stadtarchiv Halle. Grund- und Lagerbuch der Stadt Halle, 1744.
Bürgerbuch der Stadt Halle 1695, 1742.

Leiden

Universiteitsbibliotheek. Oosterse Handschriften, Archief Hamaker, Or. 5752.

London

India Office Library. Manuscripts in European Languages, Fowke Letters, MSS. Eur E6.

Norderney

Kirchen-Protocoll in der christlichen Gemeinde.

Oegstgeest

Archief Nederlandsch Zendeling Genootschap.

Utrecht

Universiteitsbibliotheek. Handschriften en Oude Drukken, Opuscula in Lingua Bengali, 1480.

Jacob G. Haafner (1754–1809):
A Brief Chronology of His Life

This brief overview of Haafner's life is based on research of a wide variety of sources, which are accounted for in the edited volumes of his complete works. Also included are events pertaining to Haafner which took place after his death. Only a few of his books are mentioned here. For a complete list of publications and reprints see the list of publications.

1754	Born in Halle, May 13
1755	Moved with his parents to Emden
1765	Moved with his parents to Amsterdam
1766	Together with his father on VOC ship
1766–68	Lived with foster parents in Cape Town
1768–69	Tutor in Batavia (Jakarta)
1769–71	Assistant of a slave-holder in Cape Town
1771–72	Painter's apprentice in Amsterdam
1772–73	Travel by sea to India
1773–79	In service of the VOC ranking from assistant bookkeeper to bookkeeper
1779–80	Free-Burgher in Nagapatanam
1780–81	Private bookkeeper at the VOC factory in Sadras
1781–82	Fourth Anglo-Dutch War. Prisoner-of-war in Madras
1782	Bookkeeper of S. Popham and A. de Souza in Madras
1783	Lives in Jaffnapatnam. Love affair with Anna Wieder. Travel through Ceylon
1784–86	Bookkeeper to J. Fowke in Calcutta
1786	Travels along the Coromandel Coast. Love affair with Mamia.
1786–87	Three-month stay on Mauritius
1786–88	Return to Europe
1788–90	Travels through Europe and lives off his fortune

Jacob G. Haafner (1754–1809)

1790	Love affair with Anna Maria Kreunink
1791	Birth of Christiaan Matthias (died 1848)
1792	Birth of Jacob (died in 1794)
1795	Lost his "fortune" due to misinvestment in French bonds
1797	Birth of Jacob Matthias (died ?)
1797–1804	Pipe trader in Amsterdam
1805	Wins prestigious award of the Teylers Godgeleerd Genootschap
1805–09	Writes for a living
1806	Publication of his first book
1806–21	Translations of Haafner's books into German, French, English, Danish, and Swedish
1807	Publication of *Examination of the Usefulness of Missionaries and Missionary Societies*, a critical treatise on missionaries and missionary societies
1808	Publication of his magnum opus *Travels in a Palanquin*
1808	Marriage with A.M. Kreunink
1809	Dies of angina pectoris in Amsterdam, 4 September
1820–22	C.M. Haafner publishes two more of his father's travelogues
1823	C.M. Haafner publishes Jacob's rendering of the *Ramayana*
1826–27	Republication of four of Haafner's travelogues.
1992–97	Integral republication of his travelogues and *Examination*.

List of Publications by Jacob Haafner

The publications are listed chronologically per language.

Note that Jacob Gotfried Haafner was born "Jacob Gotfried Haffner"; he changed the spelling shortly after his return to the Netherlands in the 1890s to avoid confusion with a neighbor whose name was "Haffner". His son Christiaan Matthias further changed the spelling of his own name to "Hafner". While different variations are used in the literature, this volume has used the standard spelling "Haafner" when not directly quoting texts.

Dutch

"Dichterlijke beschrijving van den regenmousson, op de kusten van Malabaar en Coromandel; van eene droogte, of dor jaar; en van een vreselijken hongersnood in Bengalen", *Algemeene Vaderlandsche Letteroefeningen* 1801, II, 654–62.

"Iets, over het eiland Ceilon", *Algemeene Vaderlandsche Letteroefeningen* 1801, II, 535–8, 566–72, 620–30; 1802, II, 36–46.

Lotgevallen op eene reize van Madras over Tranquebaar naar het eiland Ceilon, Haarlem 1806.

Onderzoek naar het nut der Zendelingen en Zendeling-Genootschappen, Haarlem 1807. Verhandelingen raakende den Natuurlijken en Geopenbaarden Godsdienst uitgegeven door Teylers Godgeleerd Genootschap XXII.

"Verhaal van een vreeselijken hongersnood door de Engelschen in Bengalen verwekt", *Algemeene Vaderlandsche Letteroefeningen* 1807, II, 316–25.

Reize in eenen Palanquin, of Lotgevallen en merkwaardige aanteekeningen op eene reize langs de kusten Orixa en Choromandel, Amsterdam 1808. 2 vols.

Reize te voet door het eiland Ceilon, Amsterdam 1810.

Lotgevallen en vroegere zeereizen van Jacob Haafner, Amsterdam 1820. Edited by C.M. Haafner.

Reize naar Bengalen en terugreize naar Europa, Amsterdam 1822. Edited by C.M. Haafner.

Proeve van Indische Dichtkunde volgens den Ramaijon, Amsterdam 1823. Edited by C.M. Haafner.

Onderzoek naar het nut der Zendelingen en Zendelings-Genootschappen, Amsterdam 1823. Second edition edited by C.M. Haafner.

Lotgevallen op een reize van Madras over Tranquebaar naar het eiland Ceilon, Amsterdam 1826.

List of Publications by Jacob Haafner

Reize te voet door het eiland Ceilon, Amsterdam 1826.

Reize in eenen Palanquin, Amsterdam 1827. 2 vols.

Kampen, N.G. van, *Bloemlezing uit Nederlandsche Prozaschrijvers van de zestiende tot de negentiende eeuw* (derde deel), Haarlem 1835, 1–44. Selection from Haafner's writings.

Reize in eenen palanquin, Amsterdam 1851. This third edition is a reprint of the second edition.

Reize te voet door het eiland Ceilon, Haarlem 1852. Pocket-edition.

Haafner's reisavonturen, voor jonge lieden bewerkt, Zwolle 1886. Edited by R. Koopmans van Boekeren for a young audience.

Roof en verwoesting van onze koloniën waar liefde en welvaart woonden, Voorburg, 1940. Edited by E.A.P. Dzur. Reprint of *Lotgevallen op eene reize van Madras over Tranquebaar naar het eiland Ceilon*.

"Toestanden in Batavia", en "Regering en beambten op Java", in: R. Nieuwenhuis (ed.), *Wie verre reizen doet. Nederlandse letterkunde over Indonesië van de compagniestijd tot 1870* (Amsterdam 1975), 83–93, 92–7.

De Werken van Jacob Haafner 1, Zutphen 1992. Edited by J.A. de Moor en P.G.E.I.J. van der Velde. Serie Werken van de Linschoten Vereeniging XCI.

"Selection of Haafner's Writings and illustrations", in: G. Heemskerk, J.A. de Moor, M. Salverda en P. G.E.I.J. van der Velde (eds.), *Uit Menschlievendheid zoude ik Barbaar kunnen worden. Reizen in Azië 1770–1830* (Amsterdam 1992), 16–69. Schrijversprentenboek 32.

Verhandeling over het Nut der Zendelingen en Zendelings-Genootschappen, Hilversum 1993. Annotated third edition by J.A. de Moor en P.G.E.I.J. van der Velde.

De Werken van Jacob Haafner 2, Zutphen 1995. Edited by J.A. de Moor en P.G.E.I.J. van der Velde. Serie werken van de Linschoten Vereeniging XCIV.

De Werken van Jacob Haafner 3, Zutphen 1997. Edited by J.A. de Moor en P.G.E.I.J. van der Velde. Serie Werken van de Linschoten Vereeniging XCVI.

De Werken van Jacob Haafner 1, Zutphen 1997. Edited by J.A. de Moor en P.G.E.I.J. van der Velde. Serie Werken van de Linschoten Vereeniging XCI. Second unaltered edition.

"Jacob Haafner (1754–1809). Lotgevallen en vroegere Zeereizen (fragment)", in: A. Birney (ed.), *Oost-Indische inkt. 400 jaar Indië in de Nederlandse letteren* (Amsterdam 1998), 47–57.

Jacob Haafner, "Klerkenwerk in Negapatnam" en "Moeder mist haar zoon", in: Vibeke Roeper en Roeloef van Gelder (eds.), *In dienst van de Compagnie. Leven bij de VOC in honderd getuigenissen (1602–1799)* (Amsterdam 2002), 182–3, 277–8. These are translations into modern Dutch of two small parts of Haafner's book *Lotgevallen en vroegere zeereizen van Jacob Haafner volgens deszelfs nagelaten papieren uitgegeven door C.M. Haafner*, Amsterdam 1820. They deal with the boredom of the work of a clerk at a VOC factory in India and with the misconceptions about the nature of the Dutch colonies.

Jacob Haafner, *Exotische liefde* (Amsterdam: Singel Uitgeverijen 2011). This is a rendering of *Reize in eenen Palanquin* by the author Thomas Rosenboom in contemporary Dutch.

Wie onder palmen leeft. De sublieme wereld van Jacob Haafner (1754–1809) (Amsterdam: Bert Bakker 2008).

Wie onder palmen leeft. De sublieme wereld van Jacob Haafner (1754–1809) (Amsterdam: Pallas Publications 2011). A reprint of the 2008 edition.

German

Eine Reise vion Madras nach Ceylon, Weimar 1806. Translated by T.F. Ehrmann. Bibliothek der neuesten und wichtigsten Reisebeschreidbungen, Band 3.

Landreise langs der Küste Orixa und Kormandel auf der westlichen Indischen Halbinsel, Weimar 1809. Vertaling van *Reize in eenen Palanquin* door T.F. Ehrmann in de Bibliothek der neuesten und wichtigsten Reisebeschreibungen, Band 39.

Landreise langs der Kuste Orixa und Kormandel auf der westlichen Indischen Halbinsel, Wien 1810. Austrian edition of the 1809 Weimar edition.

Fussreise durch die Insel Ceilon, Magdeburg 1816. Translated by J. Chr. L. Haken.

"Berabeite Reisegeschichten von Jacob Haafner", in: C.A. Fischer (ed.), *Die drei Ostindienfahreer, abentheuerliche Reisegeschichten,* Leipzig 1817, 5–186. This book contains a summary of *Lotgevallen op eene Reize van Madras naar het Eiland Ceylon; Voetreis door het eiland Ceylon* and *Reize in eenen Palanquin.*

"Des Hollanders Haafner's Reise durch Ceilon und langs der Ostkuste von Hindostan", in: Wilhelm Harnisch (ed.), *Die wichtigsten neueren Land- und Seereisen fur die Jugend und andere Leser bearbeitet* (Leipzig: Verlag von Gerhard Fleischer 1830). Neue wohlfeile ausgabe. In Commission bei Adolf Frohberger.

Eine Reise von Madras nach Ceylon; Britischer Raub und Verwüstung Niederländischer Kolonien, Voorburg 1941. German translation of the National Socialist edition of E.A.P. Dzur.

Eine Reise von Madras nach Ceylon; Abenteuer zu Lande und auf See, Voorburg 1943. Reprint of the 1941 edition under a different title.

Reise in einem Palankin. Erlebnisse und Begebenheiten auf einer Reise längs der Koromandelküste Südindiens (Mainz: Gutenbergbuchhandlung 2003). Translated by Thomas Kohl.

Reise nach Bengalen und Rückreise nach Europa (Mainz: Gutenbergbuchhandlung 2004). Translated by Thomas Kohl.

Reise zu Fuß durch die Insel Ceylon (Mainz: Gutenbergbuchhandlung 2004). Translated by Thomas Kohl.

Erlebnisse und frühere Seereisen (Mainz: Gutenbergbuchhandlung 2006). Translated by Thomas Kohl.

Von Madras nach Ceylon (Mainz: Gutenbergbuchhandlung 2006). Translated by Thomas Kohl.

English

Travels on Foot through the Island of Ceylon, London 1821. Translated by Sir R. Philips.

"Haafner's account of Ceylon", *Ceylon Literary Register* V, 1890–91: 82–5, 91–3, 99–100, 107–9, 114–16. This is an edited version of "Notice sur l'Isle de Ceilan".

A Journey on Foot through Ceylon, Colombo 1926–27. This translation by L.A. Prins en J.R. Toussaint of *Reize te voet door het eiland Ceylon* appeared as a series in supplements to the following editions of *Journal of the Dutch Burgher Union of Ceylon*, 15 (1926): 4, 1–14; 16 (1926): 1, 15–37; 16 (1926): 2, 39–72; 16 (1926): 3, 73–119; 16 (1927): 4, 121–42; 17 (1927): 1, 143–67; 17 (1927): 2, 169–85.

Travels on Foot through the island of Ceylon, New Delhi 1995. Reprint of the London 1821 edition.

Jacob Haafner's Description of Mauritius 1786–1787, translated by Rosemary Robson-McKillop, in: Paul van der Velde, *"Champ de Vénus" on "Roller Island". Jacob Haafner's description of Mauritius, 1786–1787* (Port Louis: The Hassam Toorawa Trust 2004), 14–23. Occasional Paper 6. Societe de l'Histoire de l'Ile de Maurice.

French

Voyages dans la pénninsule occidentale de l'Inde et dans l'ile de Ceilan, Paris 1811. (2 dln). Translation of *Lotgevallen op eene reize van Madras over Tranquebaar naar het eiland Ceilon* by M. Jansen. Also contains "Notice sur l'Isle de Ceilan", which is a translation of "Iets, over het eiland Ceilon".

Swedish

J. Haafners Landresa langs med Orixas och Koromandels kuster, Stockholm 1810–11. Translated from the German Weimar edition by C. Phil. Utterstrom.

Danish

Fodreise igiennem Ceilon, Kobenhavn 1821. Translated by Jacob Riise from the German Magdeburg 1816 edition by J. Chr. L. Haken.

List of Publications on Jacob Haafner

This is a bibliography of the writings on Jacob Haafner which also includes poems inspired by Haafner.

Dutch

Aa, A.J. van der, *Biographisch Woordenboek der Nederlanden*, deel VII, Haarlem 1867.

Adelung, F., *Versuch einer Literatur der Sanskrit Sprache*, St. Petersburg 1830.

Biografische Woordenboek der Noord- en Zuid-Nederlandse Letterkunde, onder red. van J.G. Frederiks en F. Jos van den Branden, Amsterdam z.j.

Brandt Corstius, J.C., *Geschiedenis der Nederlandse literatuur*, Utrecht 1959.

Crebelolder, Emma, *Zwerftaal*, Amsterdam 1995.

_____, "Haafner", in: J.A. de Moor en P.G.E.I.J. van der Velde (eds.), *De Werken van Jacob Haafner* 2 (Zutphen 1995), 25.

"Jacob (Godfried) Haafner 1754–1809", in: H. Heesen, H. Jansen en E. Schilders (eds.), *Waar ligt Poot? Over de dood en laatste rustplaats van Nederlandse en Vlaamse schrijvers* (Baarn 1997), 105–7.

Hofdijk, W.J., "Mamia (Zijnde een uitboezeming ingeblazen door de lecture van: J. Haafner Reize in eenen Palanquin te Amsterdam bij Johannes Allart, MDCCCVIII en thans opnieuw in 't licht gegeven, vercierd met eene door R. Vinkeles gesneden plaat uyt deszelfs Tweede Deel getrokken)", *Almanak voor het Schoone en het Goede* (1840).

_____, "Mamia (Zijnde een uitboezeming ingeblazen door de lecture van: J. Haafner Reize in eenen Palanquin te Amsterdam bij Johannes Allart, MDCCCVIII en thans opnieuw in 't licht gegeven, vercierd met eene door R. Vinkeles gesneden plaat uyt deszelfs Tweede Deel getrokken)", te Leyden bij De Uitvreter MCMXCII.

Kampen, N.G. van, *Beknopte geschiedenis der letteren en wetenschappen*, deel II, 's-Gravenhage 1822.

_____, *Bloemlezing uit Nederlandsche Prozaschrijvers van de zestiende tot de negentiende eeuw* (derde deel), Haarlem 1835.

Kolff, D.H.A., "Jacob Haafners *Reize in eenen Palanquin*: een hartstochtelijk afscheid van een koloniaal ancien régime". Lecture during the occasion of the presentation of *De Werken van Jacob Haafner* 3 in the Maritime Museum "Prins Hendrik" in Rotterdam, September 27, 1997.

Laan, K. ter, "Haafner", in: K. ter Laan, *Multatulis Encyclopedie* (Amsterdam 1995).

Lange, G. de, "Dweepzieke godsdienstijver en schandelijke vooroordelen", *Teylers Musuem Magazijn* 25 (1989), 16–19.

_____, "Dweepzieke godsienstijver en schandelijke vooroordelen", Leiden 1988. Unpublished article.

Moor, J.A. de en P.G.E.I.J. van der Velde, "'De Heilige Tale des Lands'. Jacob Haafner als voorloper van de studie van het Sanskrit in Nederland", in: *Waarom Sankrit? Honderdvijfentwintig jaar Sanskrit in Nederland*, onder redactie van H.J. 't Hart-van den Muijzenberg (Leiden 1991), 86–94 en een los toegevoegde pagina tussen pagina 86 en 87.

Moor, J.A., "Jacob Haafner 1754–1809, reiziger in Azië", *Nieuw Letterkundig Magazijn* XII 2 (1994), 26–8.

Nieuw Nederlandsch Biographisch Woordenboek, deel III, Leiden 1914.

Paasman, B., "De Nederlandstalige literatuur van en over Zuid-Afrika in de Compagniestijd", *Indische Letteren* 18 (2003), 2, 59–68, 65/66.

Prinsen, J., *Handboek tot de Nederlandsche Letterkundige Geschiedenis, 's-Gravenhage 1928.* (Amsterdam: Atheneum – Polak & Van Gennep 2002).

Terpstra, H., "Jacob Haafner en zijn denkbeelden over het kolonialisme", *Tijdschrift voor Geschiedenis* 75 (1962) 2, 129–54.

Vanvugt, E., "Jacob Haafner (1754–1809) De 'vergeten' antikoloniaal", in: E. Vanvugt, *Nestbevuilers. 400 jaar Nederlandse critici van het koloniale bewind in de Oost en de West* (Amsterdam 1996), 68–73.

Velde, P.G.E.I.J. van der, "J.G. Haafner", in: Salverda, M. (ed.), *Uit menschlievendheid zoude ik barbaar kunnen worden. Reizen in Azië 1770–1830* (Amsterdam 1992), 16–69.

_____, "Kees, Kees! riep het oranjegepeupel", *NRC*, 29 April 1999.

Velde, P.G.E.I.J. van der and J.A. de Moor, "Biografische schets van Jacob Gotfried Haafner (1754–1809)", in: J.A. de Moor en P.G.E.I.J. van der Velde (eds.), *De Werken van Jacob Haafner* 1 (Zutphen 1992), 11–38.

_____, "Uit menschlievendheid zoude ik barbaar kunnen worden. Reisverslagen van Jacob Haafner (1754–1809)", *Museummagazine Vitrine* 5 (1992), 2, 16–17.

_____, "Jacob Haafner (1754–1809) en de zending", in: J.A. de Moor en P.G.E I.J. van der Velde (eds.), *Jacob Haafner. Verhandeling over het nut der zendelingen en zendelings-genootschappen* (Hilversum 1993), 9–28.

_____, "Een zekeren Oosterschen gloed. Twee eeuwen Haafner en de kritiek", in: J.A. de Moor en P.G.E.I.J. van der Velde (eds.), *De Werken van Jacob Haafner* 2 (Zutphen 1995), 11–28.

_____, "Jacob Haafner aan het Comité voor den Oost Indischen Handel en Bezittingen", *Tmesis* 5 (1995), 5–14.

_____, "De wereld volgens Jacob Haafner", in: J.A. de Moor en P.G.E.I.J. van der Velde (eds.), *De Werken van Jacob Haafner* 3 (Zutphen 1997), 11–25.

_____, "Grote God! Wat een toestand! Het leven van Jacob Haafmner: één grote sublieme ellende", in: Rick Honings en Olf Praamstra, *Ellendige levens. Nederlandse schrijvers in de ngentiende eeuw* (Hilversum: Verloren 2010).

Vogel, J. Ph., "Jacob Haafner. Schets uit de laatste jaren der Oost-Indische Compagnie", *Indische Gids* 22 (1900), 383–407.

Vloten, J. van, *Beknopte geschiedenis der Nederlandsch letteren van de vroegste tijden tot op heden voor gebruik op Hoogere Burger- en andere scholen en alle verdere belangstellenden*, Tiel 1863.

Walch, J.L., *Nieuw Handboek der Nederlandse Letterkundige Geschiedenis*, Den Haag 1947.

Winkel, J. te, *De ontwikkelingsgang der Nederlandse Letterkunde*, deel VI, Haarlem 1925.

Witsen Geysbeek, P.G., *Algemeen Noodwendig Woordenboek der Zamenleving*, Haarlem 1836.

Zonneveld, P. van, "Een échte antikoloniaal: Jacob Haafner (1754–1809)", in: Theo D'haen en Gerad Termorshuizen (eds.), *De Geest van Multatuli. Proteststemmen in vroeger Europese koloniën* (Leiden 1998), 19–29.

English

Bibliotheca Brittannica or a General Index to British and Foreign Literature, Volume I, Authors (K. Watt, ed.), Edinburgh/London 1829.

Bor, Joep, "Mamia, Ammani, and other Bayadères. Europe's portraits of Indian Temple Dancers", in: Martin Clayton and Bennett Zon (eds.), *Music and Orientalism in the British Empire, 1780s–1940s* (Routledge: London 2007), pp. 13–52.

Ferguson, D., "Haafner's account of Ceylon", *Ceylon Literary Register* V (1890–91), 82–5, 91–3, 99–100, 107–9, 114–6.

Hooft, Hendrik, "Jewels in His Head", in: Hendrik Hooft (ed.), *Patriot and Patrician. To Holland and Ceylon. In the Steps of Hendrik Hooft and Pieter Ondaatje, Champions of Dutch Democracy*. Science History Publications/USA: Canton 1999, pp. 87–106.

Scobie, Claire, *The Representation of the Figure of the Devadasi in European Travel Writing and Art from 1770 to 1820 with Specific Reference to Dutch Writer Jacob Haafner* (Sydney 2013).

Toussaint, J.R., "Jacob Haafner, a sketch of his life", *Journal of the Dutch Burgher Union of Ceylon* 17 (1928), 3, 93–105.

Velde, P.G.E.I.J. van der, "The Orientalist, Artist and Writer J. G. Haafner (1755–1809)" , *Dutch Crossing* 39 (December 1989), 88–95.

_____, "Jacob Haafner in Mauritius, 1786–1787: Houses and Morals on Rollers", in: Sandra T.T. Evers and Vinesh Y. Hookoomsing (eds.), *Globalisation and the South-West Indian Ocean* (Réduit 2000), 117–127.

Velde, P.G.E.I.J. van der en J. A. de Moor, "Jacob Haafner. Travels Through the Island of Ceylon in 1783", in: *Journal of the Dutch Burgher Union of Ceylon* 66 (1992), 3–21.

_____, "The Curse of the Missions: Jacob Haafner (1754–1809) on Colonialism and the Christian Missions", in: William Z. Shetter and Inge van der Cruysse (eds.), *Contemporary Explorations in the Culture of the Low Countries* (Lanham 1996), 301–8.